The Earthquake & 7 Seals

The Apocalypse Begins!
Truths for Survival

Dr. Richard Ruhling

The Earthquake

&

The Seven Seals

The Apocalypse Begins

Truths for Survival

Copyright © 2015, Richard Ruhling

Published by Richard Ruhling at Kindle

About the Author

Dr. Richard Ruhling is a retired physician who was Assistant Professor of Health Science at Loma Linda University, 1974-78. He was board-certified in internal medicine and authored *Why You Shouldn't Ask Your Doctor.*

Ruhling promotes a positive lifestyle as real healthcare in contrast to prescription drugs. that are a leading cause of illness, disability and death.

Ruhling attended a Bible college and later a Bible prophecy conference in Lincoln Nebraska that was a turning point to serious interest in topics we don't usually hear about in
church.

He is available for health seminars and speaking on book topics that relate to end-time Bible prophecy with focus on the wedding parables and a time of judgment.
Egypt enslaved Israel and threw their babies in the river. The US has enslaved most people in alcohol, tobacco, drugs that we call 'healthcare' and we have aborted 60 M babies. We deserve and will get judgment like Egypt did.
Ruhling may be contacted for speaking by email or phone, Ruhling7@juno.com 928 583 7543.

Introduction

With billions of people witnessing the fragmentation of society and governments worldwide, the end-times have to be on our minds.

Some have believed the end-times were already here, but wars, famines, pestilence and earthquakes have existed for thousands of years—why are "end-times" now?

Partly because there is a crescendo or intensifying of all of the above and there is no need to document that here.

An earthquake initiates the end-times as seen in Joel 2:10,11; Zephaniah 1:7,10; Zechariah 14:1,5; 1Thessalonians 5:1-3; and in Revelation 3, the last lukewarm church of Laodicea ended in an earthquake circa 63 AD—type and antitype!

So how shall we now live in the end-times?

Our Need of a Covenant

"What is to come has been already, and God summons each event back in its turn." Ecclesiastes 3:15, New English Bible

The history we most need to understand is the Exodus because Paul included it in "all these things happened to them for examples...ends of the world." 1Corinthian 10:1,11

God took Israel through calamity (like the earthquake) to a covenant and later said, "I am married to you." Jeremiah 3:14. That's what the wedding parables are about, but they are not understood—we've been asleep with our lights out as Matthew 25:5 shows.

Bible covenants were linked with 7's. Abraham gave 7 ewes to Abimelech in a covenant. God gave 7 holy convocations to Israel in Leviticus 23. The book of Revelations with 7 seals, 7 trumpets, 7 thunders is showing how God will keep His covenant, but we will need to make one.

The timing of the earthquake at [2nd] Passover reminds us that there are 7 days of unleavened bread at the time, Leviticus 23:6. But it's not about crackers. Christ said to beware the leaven--doctrines of the Pharisees.

Church leaders over the centuries have altered God's Word to make the Bible easier to chew and swallow. But only the religion that comes from God can lead to Him, so we have to take it on His terms, not ours.

The following chapters are topics emphasized 7 times as a mark of end-time truth that we must commit to (covenant).

The 1ˢᵗ Seal—the Sound of Thunder

"I saw when the Lamb opened one of the seals, and I heard, as it were the noise of thunder, one of the four beasts saying, Come and see. And I saw, and behold a white horse..." (Revelation 6:1,2).

Click to hear music that praises God' s Name:

http://www.youtube.com/watch?v=rCzd8Yqg4TM

"Glorious is Thy name!"

Outline

1. God's name is linked to "thunder" and therefore, to the earthquake.

2. Bible names have meaning; God's name means salvation.

3. God's name was removed from Scripture.

4. "What is His name?"

5. Questions/Discussion

6. Restoring His name.

7. Summary

Overview

"Thunder" in the 1st seal is linked to God's name which is the first of seven truths by which we are "sealed." In Bible translations, wherever we see LORD or GOD in all capital letters, God's name was removed. "LORD" and "GOD" are titles. Any owner of land is the landlord. We can make a god of anything. God's name was removed from Scripture in spite of seven provisions to preserve His name. It is to be restored in the end-time by 144,000 spiritual Israelites who act as Elijah. Christ said before He comes, "Elijah must truly come first and restore all things." Matthew 17:11.

Horses in the Bible were for war. God did not want His people to multiply horses. Christ rode into Jerusalem on a donkey. But the white horse in Revelation 6:2 suggests militancy for truth in the end-time. While the white horse represents seven seals that go "conquering and to conquer," in another sense, it is the first of the seven seals and represents God's name.

"Thunder" in Revelation 6:1 is a contextual link to

"name" as the theme of the first seal.

- "Father, glorify your **name**. Then came there a voice from heaven saying, I have both glorified it and will glorify it again. The people that stood by and heard it said that it **thundered**." John 12:28-32.

- John saw the 144,000 on Mount Zion "having His Father's **name** written in their foreheads and I heard a voice from heaven...as the voice of a great **thunder**" Revelation 14:1,2.

The thunder that John heard in Revelation 6:1 was the "roar" of the Lion, Revelation 4:7; 5:5. The roar is linked to an earthquake: "The Lord shall roar (Lion of Judah, Revelation 5:5)...and the earth shall shake," Joel 3:16. This roar [earthquake in Revelation 6:1] draws attention to the white horse, a message of truth, saying, "Come and see..." So let us investigate these truths, and first of all, God's name.

The Centrality and Importance of God's Name.

A. Name is who we are. Identity theft is a leading crime today and it has also happened with God's name.

B. The seal of any ruler has his name, office of authority and dominion. Name is an essential part of the seal of God. We cannot be sealed by God without knowing His name.

C. A bride must take the name of her husband. If we want to become the Bride of Christ, we must have His Father's name because He said, "I am come in My Father's name," John 5:43.

D. Name is the first focus of the Lord's prayer—"Our Father which art in heaven, hallowed be Thy name."

E. Name is implied in the 1st angel's message: "Fear God and give glory to Him." Rev 14:7. "Give unto the Lord the glory due unto His name." Ps 96:8. (Give Him His name.)

F. Hebrew names often were a message about that person. This is true of God; we need to know His character, which is what God proclaimed to Moses when He proclaimed His name—name and character go together, Exodus 34:5,6.

2. *Bible Names Have Meaning*

Hebrew parents gave names to their children that signified their character, work or message from God. Descending from Adam for 2,000 years, the names of early patriarchs had a message. Adam is "man," Seth is "replaced," Enosh is "mortal," Cainan is "sorrow" Mahalale'el means "God, the blessed One," Jared is "shall come down," Enoch is "teaching," Methuselah is "at his death the breaking forth of waters." In sequence these names say: *Man replaced [with] mortal sorrow. God, the blessed One shall come down teaching [that] at his [Methuselah's] death, the breaking forth of waters.* Methuselah died the year of the flood!

A name connotes character. "A good name is rather to be chosen than great riches." Proverbs 22:1. God has a good name because He stands behind His word, but many people don't think so. In this end-time, He is going to fulfill His word to the group of people who accept His name and principles of His government. His name represents all of His attributes--"the name of the LORD....merciful and gracious, long-suffering, and abundant in goodness and truth," Exodus 34:5,6.

God wants us to know Him and to have His character—this is really more important than simply knowing or saying His name a certain way. But in this end-time, His name and character will go together. Those who have His name will have His character. Those who are not willing to identify with a strange name supported by the best evidence, don't have His character. They remain unsealed, in contrast to those on Mt. Zion who have His name written in their forehead. Revelation 14:1.

God's Name Means Salvation

The Hebrew letters of God's name have a symbolic meaning of salvation, shown later. The Bible suggests that if we trust in His name and call upon Him by name, He will save us.

- "Whosoever shall call on the name of the LORD shall be delivered." Joel 2:32

- "The name of the LORD is a strong tower; the righteous runs into it and is safe." Proverbs 18:10.
- "A thousand shall fall at your side and 10,000 at your right hand, but it shall not come nigh you....I will set him on high because he has known My name." Psalm 91:7,14.

His word will not return void. Most of these references to His name have an end-time context—that's when His name will prove most saving. We are entering the end-time, so His name is relevant now. It means

Protection...Deliverance...Salvation!

3. *God's Name Was Profaned and Removed from Scripture*

Consider Isaiah 42:8 in these translations—

- "I am the LORD, that is my name." King James Version
- "I am Jehovah, that is my name" American Revised

Version.

- "I am Yahweh, that is my name." Jerusalem Bible

Translations have confused God's name. The preface to the Goodspeed Bible offers this explanation—"In this translation we have followed the orthodox Jewish tradition and substituted 'the Lord' for the name...wherever [the reader] sees LORD or GOD." This is true of nearly all translations!

God Feels Bad About It

Scripture says, "I had pity for mine holy name which the house of Israel had _profaned_." Ezekiel 36:21 Changing His name violates custom and Scripture: Names [proper nouns] are not translated to their meaning. President Bush was not called "little shrub" in China. Names are transliterated to give the same sound, like "Bush." Nevertheless, Bible names, especially those with the Hebrew letter, yod, were changed, in spite of Christ saying, "One yod...shall in no wise pass from the law" Matt 5:18. The yod was the first letter of God's name, and translators removed the whole name with it!

Lucifer, the highest created being, rebelled against God's government and became the devil. He hated God but could not destroy Him. So he has tried to destroy God's identity— His name. In Scripture, to know someone's name was to know that person. But most of earth's billions have little or no understanding of who God is, in spite of <u>His provisions to memorialize His name</u>. We have become comfortable with "Lord" or "God," and "the times of this ignorance, God winked at, but now commands all men everywhere to repent in that He has appointed a [time] in which He will judge [separate those who are His from] the world. Acts 17:30,31. Why should the Creator be jubilant over our use of generic titles when He asked us not to make His name empty: "Thou shalt not take the name of the LORD Thy God in vain." Exodus 20:7.

Provisions to Protect His Name

1. In Exodus 3:15 God tells Moses to say, "The LORD...has sent me unto you: this is <u>my name</u> for ever, and this is

my memorial unto all generations." [His name was replaced by the title, LORD.]

2. When a loved one dies, we remember them with a memorial stone. Grant Jeffrey's *The Signature of God* shows that 7 is God's mathematical signature. It is a mark of end-time truth, like the 7 churches, 7 seals, 7 trumpets in Revelation, and God wrote His name into the 10 Commandments on tables of stone 7 times.

3. No changes were allowed: "You shall not add unto the word which I command you, neither shall you diminish ought from it," Deuteronomy 4:2.

4. God said His people were "called by My name..." 2 Chronicles 7:14. This was especially true for prophets; many had His name as part of their names, as we will see.

5. Solomon's Temple further memorialized His name: "It was in the heart of David my father to build an house for the name of the LORD." A dozen times in this chapter Solomon mentions His name (obscured now by

"LORD"), climaxing with the purpose of the temple—
"that all people of the earth may know Your name," 2
Chronicles 6:7,33.

7. The 3rd Commandment was intended to protect and
preserve His name. "Thou shalt not take the name of
the Lord thy God in vain." [empty], but we
misunderstand it to mean swearing.

Swearing

In Bible times men called God by name as a witness to
the truth. Abimelech said, "swear unto me here by God
that you will not deal falsely with me...Abraham said, "I will
swear...and called there on the name of the LORD," Genesis
21:23,33. This is the basis of our swearing to tell the truth
in court, and perjury is basically lying after calling God to be
a witness. Trouble or calamity has followed many who have
done so.

"Thou shall not take the name of the LORD your God in
vain" (bring to nought, desolate, make empty, Exodus
20:7). If the name is changed to LORD, it is brought to

nought and made empty to those who are supposed to hallow it or praise it, but who do not know what it is. If you were God, would you feel honored or exalted by people praising your name if they didn't know what it was? To prevent our taking His name in vain was the intent of translators, but changing it to a title (LORD or GOD) prevented our *knowing* His name.

When something bad happens and someone says "God damn it!" they are not taking His name in vain—they are taking His title in vain! God is a title and it is vain or empty to ask Him to forbid what just happened. But we take His name in vain (empty) if we say "LORD" or "GOD" where those capital letters indicate God's name was originally in the Hebrew text. Using profanity has become a popular custom that has deceived us into thinking this is the primary meaning of the commandment. We're overlooking its intent to preserve His sacred name for us to know and use appropriately.

History is "His story"

In Babylon the <u>prince of eunuchs</u> changed the names of Daniel and his friends from names that meant praise to God, to names extolling heathen deities, Daniel 1:7. The devil was behind that, and he has tried to make us eunuchs [castrate us spiritually] by changing God's name.

Babylon means *"confusion."* The spirit of Babylon is to sow further confusion by changing names, especially those of Bible origin. "History repeats"—Bible translators and Christian publishers yielded to opinions and customs based on ignorance in supplanting God's name and calling it LORD.

Israel copied other nations in wanting a king and in making a visual representation of God. They knew God brought them out of Egypt and gave them their land, but they represented Him by a calf they called Baal. Oddly, Baal means "lord." Elijah thought he was the only true believer but God told him there were 7,000 that had not bowed to Baal, a generic god.

"History repeats." Approximately 7,000 times we find "GOD" or "LORD" in Scripture. They are like the 7,000 in Elijah's day who didn't bow to Baal. So wherever we see LORD or GOD in all caps, they are a silent witness as in Elijah's day that God has a name. Modern Israel has copied the world, not by worshipping a golden calf, but by calling Him "Lord," in stead of His name.

4. *"What Is His Name?"*

After asking questions that can only refer to Deity, Proverbs 30:4 asks, "What is His name?" These words reflect our need to know. Josephus, a Jewish historian at the time of Jerusalem's destruction, gives us a major clue. He describes the high priest's golden crown, "in which was engraven the sacred name [of God]...It consists of four vowels" *Wars of the Jews,* Book 5, Chapter 5, Section 7.

Some modern authorities agree. "The letters of the Name of God in Hebrew are *yod, hay, vav,* and *hay.* They are frequently mispronounced *Yahveh* ...[but] they are all vowels." Rabbi Lawrence Kushner, *The Book of Words,* Jewish Lights Publ, p. 27.

Some say those letters are consonants, but a renowned Hebrew textbook says, "Long before the introduction of vowel-signs, it was felt that the main vowel-sounds should be indicated in writing, and so the three letters, yothe, hay, waw, were used to represent long vowels" *A Practical Grammar for Classical Hebrew,* Weingreen, Oxford University Press, 1959, p. 7-8. God's name is spelled <u>yod, hay, waw [vav], hay</u>.

The above three paragraphs support God*'s name* as all vowels. His *name is said to be glorious.* Psalm 96:8 *How?*

One reason is because of the meaning of the Hebrew letters—yod, hay and vav that compose it.

1. The yod is the first letter of God's name. It is the smallest Hebrew letter and it looks like an apostrophe.

As a vowel it has the sound of "i" in Gloria and it means _hand_ as in giving, receiving or ownership.

2. The second letter of God's name is the hay which sounds like "ah" and it represents _light_ or _rain_.

3. The third letter is the vav and as a vowel sounds like "oo" in tooth. It looks like a concrete nail and has the meaning of _nail_ or hook.

The meanings of the letters suggest they are the initials of the Father (Genesis 22:8), Holy Spirit (Genesis 1:2), and the Son Psalm 2:12; Isaiah 53:4-7. God's name is glorious for its meaning depicting the role of Father with an outstretched hand, the Holy Spirit as light to guide us and the Son nailed for us on the cross.

Some Jewish people think the shama' of Deuteronomy 6:4 conflicts with this—"Hear, O Israel: The LORD our God is one LORD." But the Hebrew word for "one" is echad. It means a combined unity as when a man "shall cleave unto his wife and they shall be one flesh," Genesis 2:24. The Father, Holy Spirit and Son represent a combined unity—one in character, purpose, all-knowing, all powerful. Genesis 1 has the Hebrew word, "elohim," which is the plural word for God when He said, "Let us make man in our image, after our likeness…"

The theme of the angel's message in Revelation 14:7— "Fear God, and give glory to him; for the hour of his judgment is come" is echoed in Psalm 96:8—"Give unto the LORD the glory due unto His name." Since we are to give Him glory and His name is glorious, it means, give Him His name!

Giving God the Glory of His Name

The best of Hebrew transliterates Josephus' statement of God's name ("four vowels") as IAUA. "I" has the international "I" sound as in Gloria. [Phonetically IAUA is ee'-ah-oo"-ah.] This may be one reason the Jews "profaned" it--to avoid the heathen mocking it or laughing at them because it is so different. But you wouldn't want God to have a name like Tom, Dick or Harry; His name must be different.

Consonants [like b, d, k, or m] are made by obstruction of air flow. God's name has no obstruction like our names or characters have. His name and His character are all flow and melody. The vowel tones are pure [not diphthongs like ah-ee = I.

If we stop to think about it, we use God's name in every word we speak or write—we would have no intelligible words without vowels. It's an insight to God's character to let us use His name in our effort to communicate with others. Let's not take His name in vain, but seek to glorify Him.

We should remember His apocalyptic promise—"then will I turn the people to a pure language [margin says lip] that they may all call upon the name of IAUA." Zephaniah 3:9.

The first two letters (IA= ee-ah) were part of many Hebrew names—the prophets often came in God's name like JeremIA or ZecharIA, and we should pronounce the "i" like "ee" as they do in most countries. Elijah was pronounced "el-ee-ah," because there is no J in Hebrew. So Elia means El [short form of Elohim, meaning God] is IA. Women named Maria or Gloria have the short poetic form of God's name (IA) as part of their name. Countries like SyrIA or SamarIA also have God's name as part of theirs.

HalleluIA is an international word meaning "Praise IA" in most languages. You can read this short form of God's name in Psalm 68:4, except translators supplanted the Hebrew yod with "J" making it "Jah," where it should be IA [ee-ah].

5. _Some legitimate questions are sometimes given as excuses for not using His name:_

1. What's wrong with the name "Jehovah"?

We now know Jehovah is a fabricated name, using

the vowel sounds of the Hebrew word *adonai* [Lord] inserted into the German or French consonant equivalents of the yod, hay, vav. There is no J in Hebrew and "hovah" derives from "havvah" meaning destruction, ruin or mischief. *Strong's Concordance #1942,1943.* This is a misrepresentation of God.

2. What's wrong with the name "Yahweh"?

"Yahweh" uses English consonants [YHWH] as equivalents to yod, hay, vav, hay. Josephus said they were vowels. Yahweh has two different vowels, ah and eh, inserted into YHWH for the same letter hay.

One authority acknowledges Josephus, but construes the four vowels as two diphthongs--"One of the letters will fall away, apocopate or be _silenced_ in pronunciation and thereby be omitted in transliteration, a phenomenon called Syncope or Ellision in Greek, but these terms are sometimes also used by Hebrew grammarians." (*The*

Memorial Name Yahweh, Jacob Meyer, Assemblies of Yahweh, 1987, p 164).

To drop the yod phonetically and call it syncope or ellision is wrong. The Savior said, "one yod shall in no wise pass from the law" (Matthew 5:18). As we said above, the yod represents the Father; it should not be dropped.

3. We cannot be sure how to say His name.

When the Greeks had an unknown God, Paul told what he knew and said, "The times of this ignorance God winked at, but now commands all men everywhere to repent in that He has appointed a day in which He will judge the world" (Acts 17:30,31). We should go by the best information available, even if we stand alone. Most men in God's hall of fame stood alone.

4. Considering so many languages, God will not be picky about how to pronounce His name.

God can forgive any sin, but He will not excuse any. Neither will He excuse an unwillingness to know Him personally by name. He says, "I will turn to the people a pure language that they may all call upon the name of [IAUA]. Zephaniah 3:9. This suggests He cares about how His name is said.

"In every age there is a new development of truth, a message of God to the people of that generation. Old truths are all essential; new truth is not independent of the old, but an unfolding of it...He who neglects or rejects the new, does not really possess the old." (*Christ's Object Lessons,* 127.)

Throughout history God has chosen different ways to test His people. We must be open to truth because _He_ is the Truth (John 14:6). Past ignorance is always excusable on that basis. Present ignorance is not excusable in a time of judgment as we have opportunity to become enlightened, Acts 17:30,31.

Krisis is the Greek word for judgment in Revelation 14:7. Destiny pivots on openness to truth in *krisis,* but human instinct tends to retreat to what is familiar.

Remedy: Seek truth before the crisis; let the light shine. "Thy name is as oil…" (Song of Solomon 1:3, Jerusalem Bible; Matthew 25:10). Five foolish virgins missed the marriage because they didn't have oil. This implies they couldn't find their way to the wedding, but in a secondary sense, they may not have His. A bride must take the name of her husband.

4.   Name is not the issue; character is.

To be sealed with His name means to have His character. "The language of the Bible should be explained according to its obvious meaning unless a figure or symbol is employed." (*Great Controversy,* 599.)

In light of the above information, the obvious and primary meaning of "name" in most texts is His name,

IAUA, not His character. If we are unwilling to stand for or be identified with an odd name, we don't have His character. His name will test our character and in the end-time, they go together.

5. New Testament writers used "*theos*" and did not feel it was essential to preserve God's name.

This presumes that the New Testament was originally in Greek, an assumption that is called in question by a growing number of scholars. Here are reasons why the NT may have originated in Hebrew:

• All New Testament books were written by Israelites whose native language was Hebrew, except for Luke.
• "When they saw the boldness of Peter and John and perceived they were unlearned and ignorant men, they marveled," Acts 4:13. Would you expect "unlearned and ignorant men" to write in Greek when it was not their native tongue?
• Josephus wrote that although he far exceeded those of

his own nation in Jewish learning, he could not pronounce Greek with sufficient exactness, and "our nation does not encourage those that learn the languages of many nations."

• Greek might have been more prevalent in cosmopolitan centers like Caesaria, but it was not the language of the apostles nor the Temple.

• "The thoughts and idioms are Hebrew...If the Greek of the NT be regarded as an inspired translation from Hebrew or Aramaic originals, most of the various readings would be accounted for and understood" (Dr. Bullinger, *Companion Bible, App 94*).

• "We must not forget that Christianity grew out of Judaism...The Pauline epistles were letters written by Paul to small [Messianic] congregations in Asia Minor, Greece and Rome. These early [believers] were mostly Jews of the dispersion, men and women of Hebrew origin....The Epistles were translated into Greek for the use of converts who spoke Greek" (*Holy Bible from the Peshitta*, George Lamsa, p xi).

Christ's concern for His Father's name was greater than most Christians imagine. The *opening phrase* of the Lord's prayer says, "Hallowed be Thy name." Three times in His last prayer He says "I have manifested Your name unto the men You gave Me. .I kept them in Your name...I have declared to them Your name and will declare it" John 17:6,12,26. It is unbelievable that something so obviously important to Christ and so central to the Old Testament is not reflected by the New Testament writers.

We might conclude there has been mischief with the manuscripts. The "little horn" is likely behind this. Daniel prophesied it would "change times and laws," and Paul said, "the mystery of iniquity does already work," Daniel 7:25; 2 Thessalonians 2:7.

6. *God's Name Will Be Restored!*

"I will sanctify My great name which was profaned among the heathen," Ezekiel 36:23.

"A Lamb stood on the mount Zion and with him an

hundred forty and four thousand, having his Father's name written in their foreheads," Revelation 14:1.

Major companies today stand behind their name. "The quality goes in before the name goes on." God is going to stake the honor of His kingdom on quality—there will be 144,000 who are sealed with His name and who "had gotten the victory over the beast," Revelation 15:2. They live through "a time of trouble such as never was" without dishonoring Him, Daniel 12:1. Because they vindicate Him in "the hour of His judgment," He will share His throne with them and is not ashamed to call them brethren," Luke 12:44; Hebrews 2:11.

Those Who Have His Name

Those who are written in His book "thought often upon His name...They shall be mine, says IAUA of hosts, in that day when I make up my jewels; I will spare them, as a man spares his own son that serves him," Malachi 3:16,17.

These jewels are the *headstone*—the crown of His

spiritual temple. God's temple of truth has been rising for centuries. Luther, Calvin, Knox, Wesley—many have built upon this temple of truth which is not yet complete, but we, are given the privilege of being the headstone.

"Who are you, O great mountain? before Zerubbabel you shall become a plain: and he shall bring forth the *headstone* thereof with shouting, crying, Grace, grace unto it," Zechariah 4:7. Zerubbabel (shoot or outgrowth of Babel) and Zechariah built the second temple and they are types. Will we accept His name and be part of the headstone for His spiritual temple? This is the focal point of all those types. This temple is seen in Revelation 11:1 as it is measured or judged when God gives power to His two witnesses for three and a half years. Vs 3.

Unless we know the name of the Creator and "extol Him that rides on the heavens by His name" [Psalm 68:4] we have a generic god and Satan will one day fill the bill—

"Whose coming is after the working of Satan with all

power and signs and lying wonders and with all
deceivableness of unrighteousness in them that perish;
because they received not the love of the truth [an odd
name; it's His name that saves; Joel 2:32] that they
might be saved and for this cause God shall send them
strong delusion that they should believe a lie," 2
Thessalonians 2:9-11.

How Will His Name Be Restored?

Before the second coming, "Elias truly shall first
come, and restore all things." Matthew 17:11. It is our
privilege to share in this work of Elijah. Since God's name
means salvation, a full-page ad in major newspapers
could save most people if a mere intellectual knowledge
sufficed. But the issues are more complex. One major
factor: God's name represents His character and He has
arranged it so that they go together, Isaiah 42:8. We
share in the restoration of His name by doing what the
Bible says:

1. By no longer taking His name in vain. Wherever we see LORD or GOD (in all caps) we should restore IAUA [ee'-ah-oo"-ah] to those places where the Bible writers originally wrote His name.

2. Christ said, "Ye are my friends, if you do whatever I command you. Henceforth I call you not servants." Closer than friends in the end-time, God says, "Call Me Ishi (Husband)...call Me no more Baali" (Lord, Hosea 2:16, margin). A loving husband prefers being called by his name rather than by a word that means "Boss."

3. We help to restore His name by sharing information on this topic. It is *present truth* for now.

Summary

God will save or deliver those who call upon His name. Many texts emphasizing God's name have an end-time context. His name symbolizes the members of Deity and was changed by translators to a generic title, LORD or GOD. The 3rd commandment forbids taking His name empty or in vain.

The names of Daniel and his friends were changed in Babylon. The spirit of Babylon is behind the changing of Bible names. Many of the Hebrew prophets came with God's name as a part of theirs. Elijah had a special role in turning Israel from the false worship of Baal, a name that meant "lord," Hosea 2:16, margin.

Josephus and modern authorities say God's name consists of four vowels; ee-ah-oo-ah, represented by IAUA. God has pity for His name and will sanctify it (Ezekiel 36:23). Appeals to ignorance won't do if we can know better. God's name will be restored by an Elijah movement that results in 144,000 having God's name as a seal or mark of protection for the time of trouble. They will be specially honored in heaven, Revelation 14:1-3.

The 2nd Seal—the Covenant

"When He had opened the second seal, I heard the second creature say, Come and see. And there went out another horse that was red: and power was given to him that sat thereon to take peace from the earth, and that they should kill one another: and there was given unto him a great sword" Revelation 6:3,4.

Taking peace from the earth is the result of God's people making a covenant with Him as suggested: *"Behold, I make a covenant...I will do marvels...I drive out before you the Amorite and the Canaanite..."* Exodus 34:10,11.

The Lord's Prayer says, "Thy kingdom come" eand when we make a covenant, we become His kingdom as Israel did in Exodus 19:5,6. Cllck to hear our Lord's prayer: http://www.youtube.com/watch?v=TAFj2-u2cGQ

When Israel became God's kingdom by agreeing to

the covenant, God took down the other nations and exalted Israel so that by the time David was king, they were the greatest nation.

We are living in the time when the kingdoms in Daniel 2 are beginning to crumble, and "in the days of these kings shall the God of heaven set up a kingdom." We can have a part in this process!

Outline

1.   History is Prophecy for 7 Years of Trouble

2.   The Covenant Takes Peace from the Earth.

3.   The U.S. Role in the New World Order

4.   Reasons to Leave the Cities

1. _History is Prophecy for 7 Years of Trouble_.

Examples suggesting a 7-year time of trouble include:

1. The 7-year famine in Joseph's time. "*The dream was doubled unto Pharaoh twice*" Genesis 41:32. Some Bible students believe that when God emphasizes something twice, it's a clue for a second, end-time application.

2. The 7 years of Nebuchadnezzar eating grass suggests an end-time humbling of this world's kingdoms. Daniel 4; Daniel 2:45

3. The 7 times hotter for the 3 Hebrews in the fiery furnace foretells "*the fiery trial which is to try you,*" 1 Peter 4:12. "Times" in Daniel can mean years, Daniel 4:19.

4. The conquest of Jericho is a type for the fall of Babylon in the end-time, 1 Corinthians 10:11. Six trips around Jericho in six days blowing a trumpet each day prefigures the six trumpets in Revelation 8 and 9, followed by the 7th day with 7 trips representing the 7 last plagues of Revelation 16, "*each day for a year,*" Ezekiel 4:6.

5.   There are two 3½ year periods in the book of Revelation: "Rise and measure the temple...and I will give power unto my two witnesses...1260 days (3 ½ years). "*When they have finished their testimony, the beast that ascends out of the bottomless pit shall make war against them,*" Revelation 11:1,3,7.

The next mention of the beast out of the bottomless pit is Rev 17:8 where we see it ridden and guided by a woman named Babylon for the last 3 ½ year period when "*power was given him to continue 42 months,*" Revelation 13:5.

This second 3 ½ years is after the deadly wound (caused by the Protestant Reformation) is healed. In the first 3 ½ years, the 2 witnesses "*have power to shut the heaven.*" Revelation 11:6.

The Elijah application brings economic drought in the 1st trumpet when the grass is burned up, Revelation 8:7. Grass represents riches, James 1:11, KJV. Elijah's drought ended in a confrontation when his prayer brought fire from heaven to show that IAUA was God, 1 Kings 18:37-39.

In the end-time, after the first 3 ½ years, the lamb-like beast [the United States, explained later] brings fire from heaven ending economic drought and causing everyone to accept the New World Order [image of Old World Order beast, Rev 13:14].

The seals are a collection of topics that God has emphasized 7 times. We saw in the first seal that His name was written on tables of stone 7 times. We now consider the word "covenant," a word found 7 times in Genesis 9 where a covenant was first made with Noah.

Bible covenants were linked to 7's, like the 7 ewe lambs that Abraham gave to Abimelech in making a covenant, Genesis 21:27,28, or the 7 holy convocations that God gave to Israel in making a covenant with them, Leviticus 23.

•Revelation is a book of 7's, and it shows how God will

keep His covenant in the end-time. As we consider making a covenant to become part of His kingdom in the end-time, we will look at those things that are emphasized 7 times to include them.

•In Daniel 12:7, Christ swears. The Hebrew word, *shaba,* means He says it seven times as in an oath or covenant, This swearing is His renewing of the covenant to give His people the kingdom in the end-time.

•All of this to suggest our making a covenant and giving God the 7's--the things He has emphasized 7 times in Scripture. We saw His name as #1. Willingness to covenant is #2 and we need to consider aspects of it...

God said to Israel, "Return...I am married to you" Jeremiah 3:14. He regarded the covenant as a type of marriage and in Numbers 6, we find a 7-fold blessing for those that choose to be set apart or consecrated to God's service.

1. The Lord [IAUS] bless you

2. And keep you.

3. [IAUA] make His face to shine upon you

4. And be gracious unto you.

5. [IAUA] lift up His countenance upon you,

6. And give you peace,

7. And they shall put My name on the children of
   Israel

2. <u>The Covenant Takes Peace from the Earth</u>

God took Israel from calamity to Mt. Sinai and **when
they covenanted to be His people and they became His
kingdom, Exodus 19:5,6**. But when Moses came down
from the mountain, they had already broken the
covenant and Moses broke the tables of stone to show
what they had done. We want God to write His law in

our hearts so we will want to do the right thing, but we need a better understanding of what His law is, which will be our next consideration in the third seal.

After Israel broke the first covenant, **God made a second covenant in which He promised to drive out Israel's enemies,** Exodus 34:10,11, "*it is a terrible thing that I will do with you*" to drive out the inhabitants of the Promised Land.

In Genesis 22, God shows the end of militant Islam when Isaac was saved from sacrifice by a ram caught by its horns in a bush. Islam teaches that Ishmael was spared by sacrificing the ram, and they celebrate it in Al-Adha. Which is right? Read about it in the left column at **http://www.americainprophecy.me**/

3. *The United States' Role in the New World Order*

The United States is the lamb-like (second) beast in Revelation 13. A lamb was a symbol of Christ. Gentle and peace-loving above every other nation, America has been Christian. But the lamb-like beast <u>causes the world to make an image of the previous</u> <u>beast</u>. The New World Order will be an image of the Old World systems from which millions fled, coming to the New World for freedom. On the heels of World War II, the United Nations seemed like a good thing, but there is more to this iceberg than we see on the surface.

The New World Order will not look oppressive to most people, anymore than the image in Daniel 3 meant trouble. To idolaters in Babylon, the image represented their kingdom; it was the finest symbol to which they could bow or pay homage. It was a time of music and celebration, but it also brought a death sentence for three Hebrews who kept God's commandments. Exodus 20:4,5 says not to respect "*any graven image.*" The New World Order <u>will</u> require worship [worth-ship, giving worth to something that goes against God's laws], Revelation 13:15-17.

U.S. Takeover by Executive Orders

Preparation for the military take-over of the U.S. is being made on several levels. REX 84 provided detention centers, initially for illegal aliens, but now to screen potential domestic terrorists in a time of national crisis or emergency when martial law is instituted. FEMA is the "Trojan Horse" that brings military strength to "continuity of government" in a time of crisis.

The Greek word *krisis* is the word for judgment ("the time of God's judgment is come") when we face life and death situations as Daniel did. "Daniel" means God is my judge, and in that setting, we are separated from those who sell out cheap to preserve their lives, when God has a better plan to save us.

Presidential Executive Orders require no approval by congress or anyone else for six months. Executive Orders give a president the ability to declare a state of emergency and martial law. This suspends all Constitutional rights, converting our democratic form of government into a dictatorship. Since 9-11, we're losing freedoms as Homeland Security brings our Constitutional rights to an end.

David Rockefeller of the Council on Foreign Relations and founder of the Trilateral Commission, praised our media for keeping their oath not to divulge the Globalist plans to the public: "We are grateful to the...great publications whose directors have attended our meetings and respected their promise of discretion." According to Rockefeller, everything is in place for the New World Order—all we need is a national emergency to provide the basis for the Presidential Executive Orders [that have been issued] to take effect.

Colonel Ammerman [under General Schwarzkopf in Desert Storm] cited unclassified information that there are about one million United Nations troops in North America [Mexico and Canada, but mostly in the U.S. on "closed military bases" no longer needed since the "cold war" with Russia ended.]

Presidential Executive Orders

The "War and Emergency Powers Act" of 1933 enables the President to declare a "national emergency" at his discretion, and to establish his own set of laws for the land. Here is a sampling:

Order 10995—Seizure of all communications media in the U.S.

Order 10997—Seizure of all electric power, fuels, and minerals, both public and private.

Order 10998—Seizure of all food supplies and resources, public and private, farms and farm equipment.

Order 10999—Seizure of all means of transportation, and total control over all highways and seaports.

Order 11000—Seizure of all American people for federal work forces. A scholarly book shows the need to disavow citizenship in earthly kingdoms in preference to God's kingdom. (*Christian Patriotism,* A.T. Jones).

Order 11001—Seizure of all health, education, and welfare facilities, both public and private.

Order 11002—Empowers the Postmaster General to register all men, women, and children in the U.S.

Order 11003—Seizure of all airports and aircraft.

Order 11005—Seizure of all railroads, waterways and storage facilities, public and private.

Order 12919—Consolidation of all the above orders, signed by Bill Clinton, June, 1994.

Rapes, beatings and human rights atrocities by United Nations officers and UN suppression of investigation (*Washington Post,* Dec 27, 01) bring us a short step from when the "image" beast will *"cause all, both small and great, rich and poor, free and bond, to receive a mark in their right hand or in their foreheads, that no man might buy or sell unless he have the mark..."* Revelation 13:16.

4. *Bible Reasons to Leave Cities*

When God made man, He put him in a garden. After Cain killed his brother, he fled and built the first city, Genesis 4:17. In God's plan for Israel, every family had a home on the land with sufficient ground for tilling. The land provided the means and the incentive for an industrious, self-supporting life. No devising of men has ever improved on that plan. The poverty and wretchedness so widespread today is due to man's departure from God's plan.

With the industrial age, men were lured into the city for easier jobs and regular hours. But a century later we see that cities are hotbeds of crime, drugs, perversions, pornography, sex, violence and vice. Young people are especially vulnerable. Millions are caught in a web of abuses and unnamable crimes. With the record of God's hatred of vice and punishment of Sodom, we should not be surprised when calamities befall the cities.

A Model for Fleeing

In the face of His rejection, Christ warned, *"when you shall see Jerusalem compassed with armies, then know that the desolation thereof is nigh,"* Luke 21:20. Josephus records the surrounding of Jerusalem by Romans under Cestius in 66 AD. The early Christians understood Christ's warning in reference to military. They fled and were spared the siege when Titus returned in the spring of 70 AD. How about us?

Hurricane Katrina was an example of what we may expect. When warning was given to evacuate and some did not do so, they were stuck--not free to leave the city. Men with guns forced some back who wanted to leave when food, water and shelter was not as expected. The time is coming when those in the cities will want to leave, but will not be able to do so.

A Second Reason to Flee

"You shall flee, like you fled from the earthquake in the days of Uzziah," Zechariah 14:5. Writing for our time, *"their goods shall become a booty, and their houses a*

desolation....The great day of the LORD is near,"
Zephaniah 1:13,14. While that applied to Jerusalem, it is also applying in America. Some federal agencies are not funded; they get money from property seized in drug raids. Some have lost property, even if no drugs were found; no wonder Daniel represents nations as fierce beasts of prey; this includes the US government in transition from a lamb-like beast to speaking like a dragon in Rev 13:11.

If we can trust the Bible, New World Order will bring trouble. A move to the country, even in a mobile home or camper on land with water and soil for a garden could mean the difference between surviving free or being forced to take the mark of New World Order, Rev 14:9.

The Woman Flees

Throughout history, from the time that Lot fled Sodom, to when Protestants braved the seas, and later the wilds of the new world, God's people have found refuge in wilderness places. In Revelation 12, after the woman gives birth to the child [which in our time may represent God's movement in the final generation], the woman flees to the wilderness where she has a place of protection for 3 ½ years. The earthquake is the second of two signs to flee. If we don't have a country place, we should seek one before fall. "*Pray that your flight be not in winter...*" Matthew 24:20.

"*When ye shall see the abomination of desolation spoken of by Daniel the prophet...flee to the mountains.*" Matthew 24:15. Further explanation of this abomination will be given later.

Though it means some hardships, country living is a protection, and God will help His people there. "*The earth helped the woman,*" Revelation 12:16. The cities are fast-filling their cup of iniquity.

The Second Message:

In our introductory chapter, we said the earthquake's message is, "Fear God and give glory to Him, the time of

His judgment is come." This is the first of three messages in Revelation 14. We now see the 2nd message, *"Babylon* [meaning the confused systems of society] *is fallen,"* Revelation 14:8.

This is so important that it is re-stated in Revelation 18:2,4—*"Babylon the great is fallen...Come out of her, my people, that ye be not partakers of her sins and that ye receive not of her plagues."* A humble home in the hills, or a secluded cabin can help provide protection and survival.

"Sell what you have"

A rich young ruler came to Christ and asked what he needed to do to have eternal life. The Savior said he should keep the commandments. The young man said that he had, and he asked what he lacked. Christ said, *"go and sell what you have and give to the poor, and you shall have treasure in heaven: and come and follow me."* Matthew 19:21.

This was an opportunity for a close personal relationship, but when the young man heard it, he went away sorrowful: for he had great possessions. Then Christ said, "*It is easier for a camel to go through the eye of a needle, than for a rich man to enter into the kingdom of God,*" Matthew 19:20-24. This includes selling what we have to be prepared.

This is linked to the richest promise in Scripture— "*Blessed is that servant, whom his lord when he comes shall find <u>so doing</u>. Truly...He will make him ruler over all that he has,*" Luke 12:43,44. "So doing" what? This promise begins with the same instruction to sell--

"*Fear not, little flock [remnant of sheep at the end of time] for it is your Father's good pleasure to give you the kingdom. <u>Sell that you have</u>, and give alms; provide yourselves bags which wax not old, a treasure in the heavens that fails not, where no thief approaches neither moth corrupts. For where your treasure is, there will your heart be also,*" Luke 12:32-34.

Conventional wisdom tends to accumulate possessions, as if our worth or security is in some way related to what we have. *"Let this mind be in you which was also in Christ..."* Philippians 2:5. He could easily have come "loaded" with everything necessary to change the world. But he emptied himself. We know the history, but we forget the message—"Follow Me!"

Summary: The 2nd Seal is about making a covenant which will take peace from the earth and the beginning of this may be seen by "*the abomination standing where it ought not*" (Mark 13:14) that the early believers understood to mean military. When we see martial law being set up, we should flee the cities as Christ said or face serious trouble.

If we wait till we see it being set up, we might be like a Presbyterian Pastor, Tom___ who carried his backpack loaded in his car to work so he could be obedient to Christ, not even returning to his home to get his things, Matthew 24:17.

But if we plan ahead, we can move and take what we need as we move out of cities. Why not put the house up for sale and travel into the country to scout out a place? A year early is better than a day late and we probably don't have a year... "*the earth helped the woman*" Rev 12:16.

You have just finished reading information on the 2nd seal, related to the red horse and the great sword that takes peace from the earth.

The 3rd Seal—"and lo a Black Horse..."

"And he that sat on him had a pair of balances in his hand. And I heard a voice in the midst of the four beasts say, A measure of wheat for a penny and three measures of barley for a penny; and see you hurt not <u>the oil and the wine</u>," Revelation 6:5,6.

Click to hear **"The Lord is my light" for so is His law--"Thy Word is a lamp unto my feet and a light unto my path," Psalm 119, http://www.youtube.com/watch?v=KAjx-mqrTfg His law is the topic of this 3rd Seal.**

Outline

1. Famine in the Forecast; Weather and Crop Manipulation

2. "Thy Kingdom Come," Trumpets Symbolic

Overview

"They have transgressed the laws, changed the ordinance, broken the everlasting covenant. Therefore has the curse devoured the earth," Isaiah 24:5,6. Man's laws have brought the world to ruin in opposition to the benevolence and wisdom of God's law that is *"perfect,"*

Psalm 19:7. "Thy kingdom come" means to pray for His dominion and His laws that feature self-government in harmony with His principles of life, health and happiness.

Famine in the Forecast

A natural sequel to war [red horse] is famine represented by the black horse. God allows physical truths to illustrate spiritual conditions. The measure of wheat for a penny in Revelation 6:6 suggests the rationing of food. The bad weather we've seen in recent years that was blamed on the
"el nino" phenomenon has created multibillion-dollar problems. Is it just a coincidence?—

"Mystery in Alaska...At a remote facility ringed with barbed wire, a brand-new array of 36 antennas rise... This little-known Pentagon-sponsored radio-physics project, called the High-Frequency Active Auroral Research Program (HAARP), is officially intended to expand knowledge about the nature of long-range radio communications and surveillance using the fluctuating ionosphere...the upper atmosphere extending from 35-50 miles above Earth's surface." "The ionospheric research instrument (IRI) is designed to temporarily modify 30-mile diameter patches of the upper atmosphere by exciting or "heating" their constituent electrons and ions with focused beams of powerful, high-frequency radio energy... This "oblique heating" ability enables HAARP to form virtual lenses or mirrors at distances of more than 1,000 miles from the transmitter," *Popular Science Magazine*, Sept 5, 1995.

Popular Science [pg 80] shows how these radio waves can be reflected off ionospheric "mirrors" back to the Pacific Ocean. "_Weather manipulation_ may be possible by building an ionospheric heater a thousand-fold more powerful than HAARP. Differential heating of areas of the atmosphere could induce local weather conditions, such as floods or droughts, useful to the military. Smooth seas might suddenly be raked by treacherous squalls..."

"HAARP will dump enormous amounts of energy into the upper atmosphere. We don't know what will happen," says Williams [Physical chemist and consultant to the Sarnoff Laboratory at Princeton University] My concern is its effect on a global scale—you can't localize the effects. With experiments on this scale, irreparable damage could be done in a short time. The immediate need is for open discussion. To do otherwise would be an act of <u>global vandalism</u>," ibid.

Meteorologists recognize the warming currents in the Pacific Ocean have contributed to a faster jet stream and increased tornado problems. They have called it the "el nino" effect. We just haven't understood all the factors in why the ocean has been warmer. "Global warming"?

It is nice that Federal Emergency Management Administration can give five minutes of warning before a tornado hits, and money after floods, especially if you buy their insurance, but why not turn the clock back and quit the weather control experiment? Imagine being told by

the New World Order that all private food supplies must be brought
to a central place for distribution, or face *severe* penalty.

Genetic Engineering in Agriculture

A new book, *Against the Grain*, reveals a revolution in agriculture. In 1997 15% of U.S. soybeans were grown from genetically engineered seed. Projections for 1998 were 100% with a similar picture for cotton, corn, potatoes and tomatoes have lagged slightly, but this practice is catching on with "blinding speed."

Three federal agencies regulate this process—USDA, FDA, EPA. All three heads have sounded like "cheerleaders" for genetic engineering, rather than impartial judges of a powerful technology that alters the balance of nature. Furthermore, their policies indicate:

1. No public records need be kept of which farms are using genetically engineered seed.

2. Companies that buy from farmers and sell to food manufacturers and grocery chains do not need to keep those crops separate from traditional crops, so purchasers will have no way to avoid "new" kinds.

3. No one needs to label any crops, or any food products with information about their genetic origins, etc.

These policies prevent epidemiologists from tracing health effects, should any appear. This is just one facet of a complex picture. They are doing this with pesticides as well. Monsanto has a line of crops with a natural pesticide engineered into cotton, corn and potatoes. Corporate profits are great, but there are serious questions of where we are headed.

There is also "Terminator Seed" which cross-pollinates with other crops in the area so that one cannot save seed from one harvest to plant the following year. New seed must be purchased. For the sake of gain and to the impoverishing of the poor, they are corrupting what God made.

"_Hurt not the oil and the wine_," Revelation 6:6.

What does the protection for the oil and wine in this 3rd seal mean? The only other New Testament reference to "oil and wine" involves the Good Samaritan who put oil and wine on the wounds of an injured man needing help. IAUA will protect those who minister to others in times of need.

The whole world will be in a crisis; need will be everywhere. *"As the Father has sent Me, so send I you…"* He was the Good Samaritan to us; now it is our turn to help others.

Christ told that story as a summary of our duty to love our neighbor as ourselves.

"Thy Kingdom Come"

Knowing the King enables us to pray "Thy kingdom come." Kingdom means dominion of a king. Dominion means government, which usually means oppression.

But not in God's plan. When Moses brought the people out of Egypt, he said, "*I have taught you statutes and judgments, even as IAUA, my God commanded me....Keep therefore and do them; for this is your wisdom and your understanding*," Deuteronomy 4;5,6.

This message is about God's law, and it emphasizes the underlined part of our basic theme, "*Fear God and give glory to Him, for the time of His judgment is come*..." His judgment is based on His law. The context for this message is after

> "*voices and thundering and lightning and an earthquake, the seven angels which had the seven trumpets prepared themselves to sound. The first angel sounded, and there followed hail and fire mingled with blood and they were cast upon the earth and the third part of trees was burnt up, and all green grass was burnt up*," Revelation 8:5-7.

Trumpets Symbolic

If this event were literal, we would all die and have no need of more plagues because grasses include the grains like wheat. If not literal, we want the Bible to decode its symbols. James 1:9-11 (KJV) likens grass to riches. *"The sun withers the grass...so also shall the rich man fade."*

When IAUA [Godhead] delivered Israel from Egypt, They afflicted the gods of Egypt.

- Egypt worshipped the Nile; it turned to blood.

- Egypt worshipped frogs; frogs were everywhere.

- Egypt worshipped cattle; cattle got sick and died.

Money is our god—*"the love of money is the root of all evil,"* 1 Timothy 6:10. God will judge the world as He did Egypt. *"What is to come, has been already, and God summons each event back in its turn,"* Ecclesiastes 3:15,

NEB. The economy, especially the stock market, is driven by greed. Paper assets will be burnt up like the green grass when the 1st trumpet sounds.

Bad Government

The problem is deeper than money, and what's coming will be worse than Egypt. Politicians and the wealthy have tax loopholes, but most men don't bring home enough to feed their families, so wives leave babies at daycare centers and go to work. Taxes subsidize tobacco growers, and also drugs to treat tobacco diseases. Alcohol also causes high health care costs. Taxes fund abortion so women's lives aren't disrupted by choices made nine months earlier. We even support international loans to bail out other countries in default so our international bankers don't lose money for their speculation.

We're seeing the results of the little horn, (Daniel

7:25) in a nearly universal disregard for the laws of Scripture. Societies favor man-made laws that are bringing the world to chaos. In this setting the remnant have an excellent opportunity to call attention to God's law, even if we have to stand alone.

Psychiatrists say it is not our power of choice, but our genetics or maternal influence from childhood that determines our behavior. Some people think science has gotten rid of God. And many church leaders think grace has gotten rid of the law in Scripture. They misunderstand. Grace is the power to obey, not freedom to do as we please. To proclaim the hour of God's judgment is to show the fairness of His law and we join His side in the controversy between good and evil. This has a bearing on every act and motive.

God's Great Laws

Governments promise health, education, and

welfare, but they do poorly in all areas—they cannot deliver these basic needs. God's law is superior because health, education and welfare are by-products of obedience. In this time of judgment that brings our world to an end, all will see that God is benevolent. His kingdom is based on wise laws that reflect love.

We showed previously that God's name and character go together. This is why Christ taught us to pray, "Our Father...hallowed be Thy name [message of the first seal], Thy kingdom come." Kingdom is the dominion of a king and our King rules by wise, benevolent laws. All of this is involved in the message of the trumpets—a message of judgment against those who are rebellious and will not be subject to IAUA.

Isaiah said, "*they have transgressed the laws, changed the ordinance, broken the everlasting covenant. Therefore has the curse devoured the earth*," Isaiah 24:5,6. Welcome to the New World Order!

Obedience to God's Physical Laws Restores Health

The more scientists learn, the more they appreciate the amazing complexity of the human body. A shelf full of books on anatomy, physiology, biochemistry, neurology, cardiology, etc, fails to show how wonderfully we are made.

We're Designed for Self-Healing!

At the core of these wonders, God designed the body to heal itself. Cuts, burns, bruises or sprains heal. Why not more serious conditions? Coronary disease is reversible by a low-fat, low cholesterol diet and progressive exercise as shown by the cover story of *U.S. News & World Report,* Aug 6, 1990. *60 Minutes* interviewed a cardiologist at Harvard who said 90% of the patients who came to him for a second opinion before coronary bypass surgery did not need the surgery. Yet most people are convinced by their physicians first to take medicine, and later to have surgery. Adverse drug reactions have made medical care a leading cause of death, *Jour. Am. Medical Assoc,* 7-26-00, p 484. When people take several drugs and develop another symptom, they should quit one, not add one. www.LeadingCauseofDeathPrescriptionDrugs.com

About 1960 the *Journal of the American Medical Association* said a vegetarian diet could prevent 97% of our coronary occlusions. A prudent lifestyle that prevents disease enables the body to heal itself.

Could the body's power of self-healing work with cancer or auto-immune disease? Lorraine Day, M.D., chief of orthopedic surgery at San Francisco General Hospital had breast cancer that spread. Her surgeon recommended radical surgery, radiation and chemotherapy. She declined all of these and by natural remedies summarized as NEW START, she overcame cancer and regained radiant health.

S = Sunlight

N = Nutrition   T = Temperance

E = Exercise   A = Air (pure)

W = Water   R = Rest

T = Trust in God.

Her experience is not unique. For an excellent DVD & book combination, visit http://ChooseABetterDestiny.com for "Eating" DVD and "The Ministry of Healing," both for only $9.95. People have overcome cancer with a vegan diet using fresh raw vegetable juices made with a juicer. The rationale is that raw fruits and vegetables have *phytochemicals* [plant chemicals] that help the body fight cancer and other diseases. Cover story, *Newsweek*, 4-25-94.

Raw Foods, Sprouts and Seeds

Sulforaphane found in broccoli is anti-cancer, but they found broccoli seed has 50 times as much sulforaphane! Seeds that are sprouting have even more health benefit than non-sprouting seed. Carried to the spiritual realm this suggests that an idea that is coming to life in our mind [sprouting] has more value than a dormant theory. The moral to this is, eat seeds like new ideas; chew them well and meditate on them. They give new life!

God's provision was, "*Ye shall eat neither the fat nor the blood,*" Leviticus 3:17. We know fat makes cholesterol and heart disease. The blood of diseased animals can cause cancer. Why do animals get disease? Imagine if your feed was mixed with manure or rotten potatoes because it's a cheap source of protein--this happens on some feed lots. Our bodies are built from what we put into them.

Food Can Make Us Well or Sick

Junk food makes junk bodies and getting replacement parts by surgery is never as good as the original equipment. If our body has been giving us trouble, it may be because we have been giving it trouble. In some cases, we don't understand the cause, but Scripture says, *"the curse causeless shall not come,"* Proverbs 26:2.

We can become allergic to a food and suffer headaches, arthritis, gastritis, colitis, dermatitis, or sinusitis with no idea that one or more foods could be the cause.

In most of these illnesses, diet is a factor. Never mind the name your doctor gives your condition; *if he doesn't know the cause,* what you put into your body is probably a factor. Speaking from experience, we can become allergic to common foods that we have abused or overindulged. Such foods often act as stimulants to us, but we only experience their negatives when the stimulation (like coffee) is wearing off and we feel the let-down effects.

God promised if we will keep His law, He *"will take away from you all sickness and will put none of the evil diseases of Egypt [like we have today] upon you,"* Deuteronomy 7:12-15.

Conformity to the Bible's laws brings health and healing. Conformity to its moral laws does the same for strained or broken relationships.

Obedience to God's moral law means happiness

Society is at the point of ruin because of the many laws that people break every day. It's been said that we do not break laws, they break us! If we jump off a building we can expect a broken leg or worse. If we participate in extra-marital sex, the hurt is more disastrous than a broken leg.

Natural and moral laws are not arbitrary and authoritative as much as they *are descriptive and definitive*--they define health and happiness for those who live within their descriptive guidelines.

The Great Teacher in His Sermon on the Mount opened with eight qualities of happiness and linked them to the law:

"Think not that I am come to destroy the law, or the prophets: I am not come to destroy, but to fulfill [fully preach, verify]. For verily I say unto you, Till heaven and earth pass, one yod [smallest letter]...shall in no wise pass from the law, till all be [ended]," Matthew 5:17,18.

Happiness is a By-product

Are murderers happy? Are thieves, liars, or adulterers truly happy? Happiness doesn't come from doing as we please; it comes as a by-product from doing what's right.

Just as the body heals itself when we conform to natural laws, we have increased happiness and better relationships with others when we conform to biblical laws.

Think how amazed a heathen spy might have been to creep into the Most Holy Place of Israel's temple to see, not an idol studded with gems, but a law describing fairness and justice for every situation in life. Moses said, *"this is your wisdom and your understanding in the sight of the nations,"* Deuteronomy 4:6.

Freedom Within the Law

In the movie, *The Ten Commandments,* Charlton Heston brought the tables of stone down the mountain and was greeted by rioting and revelry. His classic reply was, "There is no freedom without the law!" We have come to think of the 10 Commandments as God's law, but technically that is not quite correct.

In the Bible, "law" is translated from the Hebrew word *torah*. It means the five books of Moses and includes the Ten Commandments which the Bible calls "*the testimony*," Exodus 25:21; 31:18; Isaiah 8:20. The law also includes judgments (Exodus 21-23) and statutes, most of which are in Deuteronomy, but many are found in Leviticus and Numbers. Much of Leviticus includes sacrificial laws that were fulfilled by Christ. Genesis through Deuteronomy has many case histories showing how the law was applied.

Law Defines Relationships

The 10 Commandments are like a table of contents to the law that expands Commandment 5 on relationship to parents, Commandment 7 on relationship to spouse, Commandment 10 on our relationship to things, and Commandments 6,8,9 on our relationship to anyone.

"*To the law* [five books of Moses] *and to the testimony* [10 Commandments]*, if they* [anyone] *speak not according to this word, there is no light in them,*" Isaiah 8:20. Here are a few examples—

1. *Thou shalt not bear a false witness.* Society is full of gossip and destructive talk. "*At the mouth of two…or three witnesses shall the matter be established,*" Deuteronomy 19:15.

2. *Thou shalt not steal.* Fourfold restitution for stealing was required, Exodus 22:1. Those who could not repay became servant to the one they owed until the debt was satisfied, Leviticus 25:29.

3. *Thou shalt not kill.* The Hebrew word means murder. Premeditated murder was judged as deserving of death.

Exodus 21:23 says *"life for life."* If men fought and one was killed, the other could flee to a city of refuge where he could appeal his case in the presence of the dead man's family, and the judge decided if there was malicious intent.

4. *Thou shalt not commit adultery.* If we only had the 10 Commandments, one might think homosexuality is okay. But *"thou shalt not lie with mankind as with womankind: it is abomination,"* Leviticus 18:22. This commandment was designed to protect the marriage relationship. More subtle, but also along this line, *"The woman shall not wear that which pertains unto a man, neither shall a man put on a woman's garment: for all that do so are abomination unto the LORD thy God,"* Deuteronomy 22:5. "The times of this ignorance God winked at." He's been doing a lot of winking at Christian churches, but *"He now commands all men everywhere to repent"* when we know better, Acts 17:30,31.

What we have been looking at is the government's

role in avenging wrong to make a matter right. As individuals, we are not to harbor anger or bitterness—that fills us with poison. We are to forgive others [for Christ's sake and for our own good], but government has a responsibility to execute the law. This promotes a society free of lawbreakers.

The Bible's laws did the job. Israel had no crowded prisons supported by heavy taxes. There was no such thing as prison and early parole for murder or rape. Those who face death as punishment for their sin may be more likely to repent than those who have a lawyer to find a loophole and avoid paying the penalty.

4 Thou shalt not commit adultery. The marriage relation was protected in many ways not obvious to us. Every family had a home on the land with sufficient ground for tilling. Every family member was a helping hand and there was not much time to be idle. They were isolated—no phones, cars or even horses, Deuteronomy 17:16.

Israelites wore modest, loose-fitting clothing and had untrimmed beards and hair, Leviticus 19:27. Adultery or perversions like beastiality and homosexuality meant death for both individuals if caught, Leviticus 20:10-15. Christ raised the standard when He said, *"He that looks on a woman to lust after her has committed adultery in his heart*, Matthew 5:28.

Educational Provisions

The provisions of the law for education strengthened family relationships. Every father had a responsibility to teach his sons a trade and every mother was required to teach her daughters the domestic arts of cooking and sewing, and the family worked together. There were no elementary schools or junior highs with secular teachers undermining parental authority. Moses had said—

> *"These words, which I command you this day, shall be in your heart and <u>you shall teach them</u>*

diligently unto your children and shall talk of them when you sit in your house and when you walk by the way and when you lie down and when you rise up," Deuteronomy 6:6,7.

God never intended governments to provide health, education and welfare. Today we are enslaved and taxed by government for these negatives—

1. Government "Healthcare" means drugs for everyone while congressmen get donations to their re-election by corrupt pharmaceutical companies. True healthcare is what we do for ourselves in terms of diet, exercise, rest and natural remedies that help the body to heal itself.

2. Education. "American civilization cannot survive with 12-year-olds having babies, 15-year-olds shooting one another, 17-year-olds dying of AIDS, and 18-year-olds graduating with diplomas they cannot read." (Newt Gingrich). The government's

"*Goals 2000*" plan is designed to usurp your control of your children by the "education" they receive. By the time most children reach their teen years, most parents have little input to their teen's choices. It's been happening for decades as the *LA Times,* April 4, 1994, suggests:

1. Clean the Slate: Uproot any pre-existing values

2. Dumb Them Down: Omit academics.

3. Modify Behavior: Animal training techniques

4. Confuse their Values: Dialectic Marx process.

5. Assess, Remedy: Is the program taking hold?

"If you teach them that they came from apes, they will

<u>act like apes</u>."

Evolution is actually a religion. It takes blind faith to believe in theories that conflict with one another and often theories are revised by millions of years. It takes intelligent faith to believe the Bible. Teaching that we came from apes is creating a jungle mentality. The Bible says God made mankind in His own image. It offers a better way of life and a wonderful destiny.

Government "welfare" tends to poverty. In Bible times, land went to the sons with a double portion to the first-born who had responsibility to care for his parents in old age. Since the parents cared for the children earlier, the children have an obligation to care for aged parents.

Obedience to God's laws means salvation

Paul wrote "by the deeds of the law there shall no

flesh be justified." We cannot earn salvation by our effort to keep the law, but as a standard of conduct and guideline for society, the law is indispensable.

Paul studied law under Gamaliel and said, *"the law was our schoolmaster to bring us to Christ*, Galatians 3:24. When we graduate from school, we don't kick the teacher or burn the books. We live by what we have learned.

The Law is Healing, Saving, Restoring

In Hebrew, "health" and "salvation" are the same word: *yeshuah.* It is no coincidence that this was Christ's Hebrew name. If the law brings us to Him, its nature must be healing, saving, restoring. Paul said the law kills, but that is if we try to earn our salvation by keeping it. Salvation is a free gift. Out of gratitude, we want to serve Him. Christ says, *"If you love me, keep my commandments,"* John 14:15.

Israel's beloved king David wrote the <u>formula for success</u> in Psalm 1: *"Blessed is the man... [whose] delight is in the law of IAUA; and in his law does he meditate day and night...and <u>whatsoever he does shall prosper</u>,"* Psalm 1:1-3. David wrote the longest chapter in the Bible; every verse in Psalm 119 praises God's law. It has eight verses exalting the law for each of the 22 letters in the Hebrew alphabet. Here's a sample:

> *"Open my eyes that I may see wondrous things out of Your law...I will walk at liberty, for I seek Your precepts...Horror has taken hold on me because the wicked forsake Your law...The law of Your mouth is better to me than thousands of gold..."* Psalm 119:18; 45, 72.

"<u>The law [torah] of the LORD is perfect</u>, converting the soul," Psalm 19:7. Can we improve on what God says is *perfect?* Any effort to change what is "perfect" causes <u>*problems*</u>. In fact, the problems of society are those of lawlessness—people living without reference to God's

law.

Changing God's Laws

It happened first with churchmen and then spread throughout society. The first church period was praised for hating "the deeds of the Nicolaitans" who were against the law; according to history they were "antinomian." This word also suggests anti-name; the French word for name is nom; nomenclature is a system of names. Thus, antinomian [against the law] is also against God's identity [name] because He is the author of all true law.

As time went on and change became easier, church leaders drifted with natural inclinations reflected in some Bible translations like this—"*Blotting out the handwriting of ordinances that was against us, which was contrary to us, and took it out of the way, nailing it to his cross,*" Colossians 2:14.

From this translation (and others), we could believe the law is the problem, and it was nailed to the cross. But it was the record of our sins that were nailed to the cross. There was no further need for animal sacrifices because type met antitype in the death of Christ. He is our sacrifice. God's people are split between Jews who see great meaning and value in the law of God [but do not see Christ as the Messiah] and Christians who see Him as the Messiah, but miss the value of His law.

When He taught us to pray "Thy kingdom come" He was telling us to look forward to His dominion based on His laws. Do we think He will come up with a new set of laws that we like better? Maybe in the new ones we can lie, steal, kill or commit adultery. Not a chance. He says, "*I change not*," Malachi 3:6.

God's Law Will Be Restored

This restoration is voluntary and only for those who choose Him as King. When we pray, "Thy kingdom come..." we are asking for His dominion. The *American Heritage Dictionary* has an interesting meaning for dominion. Besides control of a government, it can also mean a self-governing nation within the British Commonwealth. God's "Commonwealth" will also be a self-governing dominion based on His New Covenant promise—"*I will put my spirit within you, and cause you to walk in my statutes, and you shall keep my judgments*," Ezekiel 36:27.

Christ said that before He returns, "*Elia truly shall first come and restore all things*," Matthew 17:11. This was a dual reference to His first and second coming—He said Elia is come already, speaking of John the Baptist for the first application. The last words in Hebrew Scripture say, "*Remember the law of Moses...with the statutes and judgments. Behold, I will send you Elia the prophet before the coming of the great and dreadful day of IAUA*," Malachi 4:4,5. We can participate in restoring His laws.

Deuteronomy 28 lists the blessings that America has enjoyed, but the blessings turn to curses if we do not obey God's law. Anticipating fulfillment of these promises we should play our part—*"You shall be called, The repairer of the breach,"* Isaiah 58:12. A breach was made in God's law in ways that we are only beginning to see.

Torah Codes

Computers have helped discover Equidistant Letter Sequences [ELS]. If you start with the first Hebrew letter of "torah," the first tav in Genesis 1:1 and skip 49 letters, you come to the 2nd letter of "torah." Skipping again 49 letters, you come to the 3rd Hebrew letter that spells torah, etc.

This phenomenon is repeated in Exodus. In

Leviticus, the computers found God's name spelled out every eight letters from the 1st yod. In Numbers, the torah was spelled in reverse at a 50-letter interval, and in Deuteronomy, also in reverse at a 49-letter interval. This is called a chiasm with the last part as a mirror-image of the first, and in this case, IAUA is in the middle of it. This phenomenon has been published in mathematical journals with the probability of less than one in a million that it would be by chance.

Answers to Objections

1. An eye for an eye and life for life was the Old Testament way; but Christ said to love your enemy and forgive him.

It is true that we should forgive for our own good rather than nurturing hate. "*Vengeance is Mine, I will repay says the Lord*," Romans 12:19. It's the government that's responsible to uphold the laws of God concerning man's dealings with his fellowman—"*the powers that be are ordained of God*," Romans 13:1. He has let each nation show harmony with His law and to the extent that they have, prosperity has resulted. When government does not execute true justice, society becomes lawless. The world is falling apart because of its rebellion toward bad laws.

Objection 2. We cannot keep the Bible's laws because they are different from the laws we are under in government.

We are not responsible for our inability to avenge or bring justice on those who are let off by a weak government, but we can choose God's laws for our own standard of conduct. It is in this sense that we become subjects of His kingdom. As we choose this higher standard voluntarily, we are ready for His kingdom.

Objection 3. We are unable to keep the law. No one

except Christ has done it.

- *"Enoch walked with God and was not, for God took him,"* Genesis 5:24.
- Job was *"a perfect and upright man,"* Job 1:8.
- David: *"I have remembered your name, O Lord, in the night, and have kept Your law,"* Psalm 119:55..
- *"Abraham obeyed My voice, and kept My charge, My commandments, My statutes and My laws,"* Genesis 26:5.

We cannot equal Christ's perfect life, but we will not be approved of heaven if we do not copy His pattern and seek to emulate Him by the grace of His Spirit. He says, *"Follow Me!"*

Objection 4. The law is the "schoolmaster" that leads us to Christ, but there the role of the law ends.

"Think not that I am come to destroy the law or the prophets: I am not come to destroy, but to fulfill [fully preach, verify.] *For verily I say unto you, one yod [smallest Hebrew letter] or one tittle shall in no wise pass from the law, Till heaven and earth pass and all be fulfilled,"* Matthew 5:18. Christ was the Word [logos = doctrine or law] made flesh, John 1:14.

Objection 5. Didn't the early church decide we didn't have to keep the law?

"My sentence is, that we trouble not them, which from among the Gentiles are turned to God, but that we write to them, that they abstain from pollution of idols and from fornication, from things strangled and from blood. <u>For Moses of old time has in every city them that preach him, being read in the synagogues every Sabbath day,</u>" Acts 15:19-21.

Early believers were not excluded from fellowship—they could join as full members knowing they would have exposure to the law as it was "*read in the synagogues every Sabbath day*."

"*All Scripture is given by inspiration of God, and is profitable for doctrine, for reproof, for correction, for instruction in righteousness,*" 2 Timothy 3:16. The only Scripture in existence when Paul wrote this was the Old Testament, yet many Christians are woefully ignorant of these Scriptures and as the shallow rooted plants in Matthew 13:6, they will wither in the end-times.

Summary

Man's greatest advances have come from understanding law. Putting men in space, the use of nuclear energy, computer technology or electricity—all of these result from understanding law. Health, happiness and peace of mind also come from understanding [standing under] God's laws.

Judgment is based upon law. Law is translated from the Hebrew word *torah* meaning the five books—"*the law of Moses with the statutes and judgments. Behold I send you Elijah the prophet before the great and dreadful day*..." Malachi 4:4,5. The law is preventive, healing and restorative with provision for health, education, welfare and salvation. Those who meditate on the law day and night are promised that they will prosper. Psalm 1:1-3. Let us pray, "*Thy Kingdom* (dominion by law) *come.*"

The 4ᵗʰ Seal—"Behold a Pale Horse"

"And I looked, and behold a pale horse: and his name that sat on him was Death, and Hell followed with him. And power was given unto them over the fourth part of the earth, to kill with <u>sword, and with hunger, and with death, and with the beasts</u> of the earth." Revelation 6:8.

Music: Once to every man and nation comes the moment to decide..." The words of this hymn are awesome and true:
http://www.youtube.com/watch?v=cOGHCzuinBw

Outline

1.   Daniel's Prophecies and a Smokescreen

2.   Protestantism and Liberty Lessons

Overview

Just as IAUA's laws bring health, happiness and destiny, changing them brings death and hell. This chapter looks at the forces behind the desolation of faith for millions of people. History is "His story," and in this chapter we look at the reapplication of history.

Those who don't understand history's lesson may be doomed to repeat it. The introduction suggested the white horse in history was the early gospel that went "conquering and to conquer." It was followed by the red horse of Roman persecution, the black horse of famine and the pale horse of disease. Death decimated whole villages from the plague that swept Europe when the Holy Roman Empire (Old World Order) controlled Europe. Since Rome boasts infallibility and they do not change, there are lessons for us when New World Order is set up. We look through the lens of Daniel, the only book Christ cited when asked about the end of the world., Matthew 24:15.

God loves black and white, brown and red, Atheist and Jew, Catholic and Protestant, Hindu and Muslim. Yet millions who profess faith in the Bible know little of it because their church or group does not teach Scripture as the guide of life.

False religion has been responsible for more wars than any other cause in history. Our purpose is to reveal God's plan of wisdom from the Bible so the reader may choose the way of life and escape the coming widespread destruction..

Millions have been taught that it doesn't matter what you believe about God, just as long as you are sincere. But if you drink poison, sincerely believing it is grape juice, you'll get sick and could die. It's the same idea with what we feed our mind.

Millions trust their souls to the minister, priest or rabbi without a thought of reading the Bible for themselves. It seems as difficult for a Lutheran or Presbyterian minister to see the Bible's example of baptism as it is for a medical doctor to refer a person with back trouble for chiropractic care.

Clergy, doctors, university professors—so many

leaders of society are stuck in the confines of their training and can't see "outside the box."

When we live in harmony with God's principles, we are choosing life. When we ignore them, we deceive ourselves and play into the hands of Satan who is using the major systems of religion.

The Bible teaches us to be like the Bereans who "*received the word with all readiness of mind, and searched the scriptures daily, whether those things were so,*" Acts 17:11. Our focus will challenge many customs.

Daniel's Prophecies Simplified

When Christ was asked about the end of the world, He urged our understanding of the prophet Daniel—"*let the reader understand,*" Matthew 24:15.

Daniel 2: The king dreamed of an image of a man with

head of gold, chest of silver, waist and thighs of brass, and legs of iron. Daniel told the king of Babylon that his was the first of four kingdoms represented by the four metals that would rule the world, Daniel 2:38-44. History shows that Babylon was followed by Medo-Persia, Grecia and Rome.

The feet were made of iron mixed with clay--strength and weakness. Since the Roman Empire, there has been no world dominion in spite of efforts by Napoleon, Hitler, and others.

Then "*in the days of these kings shall the God of heaven set up a kingdom that shall never be destroyed,*" Daniel 2:44. This is about a stone that is cut out of a mountain which represents God's people--"*Jerusalem, My holy mountain.*" We can be part of that stone kingdom that smashes the image.

Daniel 3: The king of Babylon rejected the idea that his

kingdom would be superceded by another. He built an all-gold image and summoned the realm to celebrate his kingdom and bow to the image that represented his empire. This was a prophecy for America as we will see later.

Daniel 7: God gave Daniel a dream of four beasts that represented the same four kingdoms of Daniel 2. They allowed greater detail showing how history would unfold, especially concerning the fourth beast. The lion represented Babylon, (the image's head of gold), the bear was Medo-Persia (image's chest of silver), the leopard was Grecia (image thighs of brass) and the dreadful beast with ten horns (image legs of iron) was the Roman Empire.

Further detail is seen in the 10 horns that grew out of the fourth beast. They represented the 10 tribes roaming Europe that developed as the Roman Empire fell) The Francs became France, Ostrogoths were Austria, and so on. Daniel was concerned about the "little horn" that uprooted the three horns:

1.   "*He shall speak great words against the most High,*

2.   *and shall wear out the saints of the most High*

3.   *and think to change times and laws.*" Daniel 7:25.

1. <u>The Protestant Reformers</u> were united in their understanding that this was the papacy. The "*great words against the most High*" fit the papal claim of infallibility reflected by one of the pope's many titles, "Lord God the Pope."

2. He "*shall wear out the saints.*" Historians estimate 80-100 million Protestants were martyred by the papacy. Thousands risked their lives to flee for freedom in the

New World where America offered opportunity better than the papal-dominated country south of our borders.

This was foretold in Revelation, if we understand that a woman represents God's people, Jeremiah 6:2. In Revelation 12:6, "*the woman fled into the wilderness.*" The wilderness represents an unpopulated area of the world in contrast to "*the waters which you saw where the whore sits, are peoples and multitudes and nations and tongues*" (papacy in the old world, Revelation 17:15).

We understand the woman fleeing as the pilgrims who were seeking freedom from papal oppression, but we fail to see their flight as a model for us in the end-time. America's greatness has been due to a Constitution that was Protestant in nature with the government not dominated by the papacy. This division gave us basic freedoms and it explains why America has surpassed all nations south of our borders that are Catholic.

When America faced its greatest challenge and nearly lost its union by the Civil War, the pope, eager to divide America, wrote to Jefferson Davis, recognizing him as "the illustrious and honorable President of the Confederate States," an endorsement that no other country made. By the grace of God, the United States kept its union, but Abraham Lincoln paid with his life.

Lincoln's story began in Illinois with beloved priest, Father Charles Chiniquy, a man of principle. He could not go along with the bishop's scheme to gain some Illinois lands. Chiniquy's superiors planned his entrapment. He was prosecuted under false charges, but spared when a woman told young Abraham Lincoln the truth. Lincoln defended Chiniquy who later unmasked the church in his book, *50 Years in the Church of Rome.* Chiniquy wept when Lincoln won at court, because, he said he could see hatred in the eyes of the Jesuits in the courtroom, and he lamented to Lincoln that he would pay with his life.

Lincoln was already hated for speaking against slavery. "The majority of the Roman Catholic bishops, priests and laymen [were] publicly for slavery." Roman Catholic Chief Justice Tany said, "Negroes have no rights which the white man is bound to respect." This was in the Dred Scott Decision, quoted in *The Big Betrayal,* pg 55, written by Alberto Rivera, an ex-Jesuit priest who survived numerous attempts on his life, only to succumb to food poisoning.

The papacy has hated every power that does not bow to the pope. This included the Serbs who aided our downed military pilots in World War II. Papal "rat lines" aided the escape of countless Nazis, including Ante Pavelich who was responsible for the slaughter of 750,000 Serbs. The Nazis were hidden underground in Rome until they could be sent to Argentina where they were given asylum, though some were discovered and extradited for war crimes' trials. The Vatican-Nazi connection was covered by Geraldo Rivera on TV.

Weak Regret

On March 12, 2000, John Paul II expressed regret for past martyrs—"the sins committed by Catholics in the name of the church." He failed to tell the church's role, but blamed the members who were doing what they were told. Those who listened for references to the holocaust in his apology were disappointed.

His letter, *Dies Domini*, [July, 1998] urges governments world-wide to honor Sunday as "the Lord's Day" by civil laws and penalties. His 80-page document says "a violator should be punished as a heretic." 300 years ago, the burning of heretics at the stake was the most exalted form of worship for Catholics; it was called the "Auto de Fe" [Act of Faith]. Rome boasts that it doesn't change

Putting the two previous paragraphs together suggests a diagnosis of schizophrenia, a word that means "split brain." If the right brain says "we're sorry" while the left brain appeals for laws to punish heretics, psychiatrists would call it schizophrenia ["split brain"], if they didn't know it was the pope.

"*He shall...think to change times and laws.*" Dnaiel 7:25. The easiest example of this is the 2nd Commandment because images are so prominent in the church. *"Thou shalt not make unto thee any graven images..."* was eliminated, but to maintain a total of 10 Commandments, the Catholic Catechism divided the 10th Commandment into two--not coveting your neighbors wife and not coveting his goods. Catholic Bibles are good translations, but the church doesn't encourage reading the Bible for the above and following reasons:

A.   Christ said, "*Call no man your father upon the earth: for one is your Father, which is in heaven,*" Matthew 23:9. [pope = papa, and priests are called Father].

B. "*When ye pray, use not vain repetitions,*" Matthew 6:7 [rosary].

C. "*Pray ye, Our Father...in heaven.*" Matthew 6:9 [the Bible does not say to pray to Catholic saints].

D. "*Who can forgive sins, but God alone?*" Luke 5:21. [vs confessing to a priest].

E. "*Search the Scriptures...they testify of Me.*" John 5:39. Catholic people are taught the catechism, but most of them know little about the Bible. The end result is a system that desolates the Christian experience. "*Man shall not live by bread alone but by every word...of God,*" Matt **.

F. A man-made system of religion breaks God's law. It promises salvation to people who pay the priest. Its urging of good works to earn salvation is antichrist-- in place of Christ who offers salvation freely, "*not of*

works, lest any man should boast," Ephesians 2:9.
Only the religion that comes from God can lead to
God.

This information is not a condemnation of sincere
believers who are living up to the light that they have.
God has a way of bringing truth to our door and testing
whether our faith is in Him and His Word, or in man. The
condemnation is against a system of belief so clearly
exposed in Scripture.

The Syllabus of Errors and Protestant Sects

Excerpts from the book, *Roman Catholicism* by Dr.
Lorraine Boettner, The Presbyterian and Reformed
Publishing Co:

"Another trait of the Roman Church is her attempt
to brand all other church groups as 'sects,' and as
schismatic...We would define a sect as a group that

shuts itself in as God's exclusive people, and shuts all others out...On that basis the Roman Church, with its bigoted and offensive claim to be "the only true church," its readiness to brand all others as heretics, its anathemas or curses so readily pronounced against all who dare to differ with its pronouncements, and its literally dozens of heresies and practices which are not found in Scripture, automatically brands itself as the biggest and most prominent of all the sects.

"This sectarianism is shown, for instance, in statements such as the *Syllabus of Errors*, issued by Pope Pius IX in 1864, and still in full force where the Roman Church can enforce its will. The hierarchy in the United States plays down this Syllabus, and for many years has conducted a subtle campaign designed to hide many of its distinctive doctrines and so to gain favor with the American public. But here are its claims in plain language:

15. "No man is free to embrace and profess that religion

which he believes to be true, guided by the light of reason."

17. "The eternal salvation of any out of the true church of Christ is not even to be hoped for."

18. "Protestantism is not another and diversified form of the one true Christian religion in which it is possible to please God equally as in the Catholic Church."

24. "The Church has the power of employing force, and (of exercising) direct and indirect temporal power."

37. "No national Church can be instituted in a state of division and separation from the authority of the Roman Pontiff."

42. "In legal conflict between Powers (Civil and Ecclesiastical) the Ecclesiastical Law prevails."

45. "The direction of Public Schools in which the youth of Christian states are brought up...neither can nor ought to be assumed by the Civil Authority alone."

48. "Catholics cannot approve of a system of education for youth apart from the Catholic faith, and disjoined from the authority of the Church."

54. "Kings and Princes [also Presidents and Prime Ministers] are not only <u>not exempt</u> from the jurisdiction of the Church, but are subordinate to the Church in litigated questions of jurisdiction."

55. "The Church ought to be in union with the State, and the State with the Church."

"Let no one say that this *Syllabus of Errors* belongs to a former age and that it is not to be taken seriously. Even today it forms a part of the ordination vows of every Roman Catholic priest in the world." *Roman*

Catholicism, Boettner, pg 24-26.

Liberty Lessons from Great Men

Contrast papal aims with concepts of freedom that great Americans have held.

George Washington: "Any man, conducting himself as a good citizen and being accountable to God alone for his religious opinions, ought to be protected in worshiping the Deity according to the dictates of his own conscience." Reply to United Baptist Churches of Virginia, 1789.

Ulysses S. Grant: "Leave the matter of religion to the family altar, the church, and the private school supported entirely by private contribution. Keep church and state forever separate." Speech at Des Moines, IA 1875.

Note: **The U.S. Supreme Court with its Catholic appointees has broken this principle**. The use of tax money or vouchers for church schools [most of them are Catholic] is favored.

Benjamin Franklin, Statesman, Inventor, Author: "When religion is good, it will take care of itself. When it is not able to take care of itself, and God does not see fit to take care of it, so that it has to appeal to the civil power for support, it is evidence to my mind that its cause is a bad one." Letter to Dr. Price.

Alexander Campbell, Founder of Disciples of Christ Church: "There is not a precept in the New Testament to compel, by civil law, any man who is not a Christian to pay any regard to the Lord's day, more than to any other day, and is without the authority of the Christian religion. The gospel commands no duty which can be performed without faith in God. 'Whatsoever is not of faith is sin,' but to compel men destitute of faith to observe any Christian institution, such as the Lord's day, is commanding a duty to be performed without faith in God. Though the pope says to do so]...to command unbelievers, or natural men, to observe in any sense the Lord's day, is anti-evangelical, or contrary to the gospel." *Memoirs*, Vol 1, pg 528.

Charles H. Spurgeon, Prince of Preachers: "I am ashamed of some Christians because they have so much dependence on Parliament and the law of the land...we earnestly cry, `Hands off! Leave us alone.' Your Sunday bills and all other forms of the act-of-Parliament religion seem to me to be all wrong. Give us a fair field and no favor, and our faith has no cause to fear. Christ wants no help from Caesar." *Church in Politics* by Charles Longacre.

John Wesley, Founder of the Methodist Church: Condemn no man for not thinking as you think. Let every one enjoy the full and free liberty of thinking for himself. Let every man use his own judgment, since every man must give an account of himself to God. Abhor every approach, in any kind or degree, to the spirit of persecution, if you cannot reason nor persuade a man into the truth, never attempt to force a man into it. If love will not compel him to come, leave him to God, the judge of all." *Church in Politics*, Charles Longacre.

Our Constitutional rights and freedoms are a reflection of Protestant thought. Both have been losing ground for more than a century. Catholicism has taken a conciliatory course. Jesuits have laundered history by buying old books and favoring newer ones that minimize Rome's history. Most people today have little idea what America's founders fled.

There is an increasing indifference about doctrines that separate Protestants from Catholics. The opinion is gaining ground, that, after all, we do not differ so widely upon vital points as has been supposed, and that a little concession on our part will bring us into a relationship with a large segment of Christians.

History suggests that the New World Order will allow religious liberty for the masses to do as they please, while information intended to warn (like what your are reading) will be a hate crime, though this writer hates no one but the system that lives off the ignorance of its subjects.

Daniel is encoded; Revelation is revealed for endtime

Revelation 13:1-3 has imagery of a beast (cartoon to represent earthly governments) that is the amalgamation of the four beasts from Daniel 7. It has a mouth like a lion that represented the kingdom of Babylon, feet like a bear that depicted Medo-Persia. but it looks like the leopard of Grecia in Daniel 7, but also having 10 horns from the dragon.

The Protestant Reformation ended with the removal of the pope by Napoleon to France where his death (1799) "seemed to portend the dissolution of the papacy." This was the *"deadly wound,"* Revelation 13:3, but Mussolini reinstated the papacy in 1929. Since then, Evangelical leaders who have not understood the prophetic role of the papacy, have brought further healing of the wound and the death of Protestantism!

The United States and New World Order

The United States is represented by the second, lamb-like animal in Revelation 13:11. A lamb is gentle, peace-loving, and a symbol of Christ, John 1:29. The previous [papal] beast had crowns on its horns, but the second beast does not, suggesting a nation with no king and a church no pope--Protestant America.

But Revelation 13:14 says the lamb-like beast [United States] causes the world to make an image of the previous [papal] beast. The U.S. has created an image of the Old World Order when the papacy ruled the world. New World Order is centered in the United

Nations. It is the image beast and it will be like the Old World Order—

> "*He* [United States] *had power to give life unto the image [U.N.] of the beast [papacy]...and cause that as many as would not worship the image of the beast should be killed. And he causes all, both small and great, rich and poor, free and bond, to receive a mark in their right hand or in their foreheads, that no man might buy or sell unless he have the mark... Let him that has understanding count the number of the beast: for it is the number of a man; and his number is <u>Six hundred threescore and six</u>.*"
> Revelation 13:15,16,18.

One of the pope's titles is Vicar of Christ. In Latin the words are Vicarius Filii Dei, Vicar of the Son of God. The Roman numerals of the Latin words total <u>666</u>.

V =   5   F   D = 500

I =   1   I = 1   E

C = 100   L = 50   <u>I =   1</u>

A   I =   1   501

R   <u>I =   1</u>

I =   1   53

U =   5

<u>S   0</u>

    112

U counts as V for 5 in Roman numerals. 666 is the sum, and also of the Greek letters for antichrist shown in the next chapter. Since the U.N. is the "image beast," they will get along well when "the mother church" rides this New World Order beast in Revelation 17. This is the system that Satan will use to control the world.

Clues in Revelation 17 Explained: *Verses*

1. *"the great whore"*--a church with impure doctrines and teachings, based on tradition and decisions of councils.

2. *"with whom the kings of the earth have committed fornication"*—a church involved in politics and governments.

3. *"scarlet colored beast"* the color of cardinals, *"names of blasphemy"*—Lord God the Pope, claim of infallibility, etc.

4. *"decked with gold and precious stones and pearls"*—a wealthy church. The pope sent an estimated $666

million in gold to help sponsor the Boshevik Revolution to get rid of the Russian Orthodox Church, (the leader wouldn't bow to the pope) but the pope was double-crossed by the Communists who kept his gold due to the wise Russian Orthodox leader who gave them the Czar's gold, explained in *The Godfathers* (~ half way) http://www.chick.com/reading/comics/0114/0114_allin one.asp

5. *"Mystery, Babylon the Great, the Mother of Harlots and Abominations."*Babylon uses mystical interpretation, saying that the Bible does not mean what it says and only the priest can interpret it to lay people.

Alexander Hislop's *The Two Babylons* traces Catholicism's corruption by ancient heathenism. It is significant that Catholicism claims to be the Mother church. A "mother of harlots" means a mother of churches that are also corrupted by her abominations and false teachings.

6. *"drunken with the blood of saints and...of martyrs"* — 80-100 million Protestants were tortured, burned at the stake, or martyred for protest or noncompliance,.

Verses 9,18—*"the seven heads are <u>seven mountains</u> on which the woman sits...that great city."* Rome is the city of seven hills.

As Mother of Abominations, Rome is responsible for most doctrinal corruption of Scripture. We look now at a major example. Something that caused God [IAUA] much concern, enough to stress the point seven times.

<u>Sabbaths: a 7-fold Truth</u>

In Ezekiel 20:11-24 we find the statutes, judgments and sabbaths emphasized seven times. *"I gave them my sabbaths, to be a sign between me and them, that they might know that I am the IAUA that sanctify them."*

William Cooper wrote, "The 7th day, the Sabbath as handed to Moses by God, is Saturday. The celebration of Sunday as the Sabbath is verification that the people recognize the Pope as SUPERIOR TO GOD. The only WHOLE people who have not recognized the authority of the Pope are the Jewish people, and that is why the Vatican has not and will not recognize the state of Israel." *Behold A Pale Horse*, pgs 89,90.

People pay a price for plain speaking. Cooper was gunned down by federal agents on a walk to his (rural) mailbox. May we gain courage from Lincoln's immortal words, "that from these honored dead, we take increased devotion to the cause for which they gave the last full measure of devotion."

Sabbath is a Memorial to Creation

"Remember the Sabbath day, to keep it holy. Six days shall you labor, and do all your work, but the seventh day is the Sabbath of IAUA your God: in it you shall

not do any work...*for in six days IAUA made heaven and earth,* the sea, and all that in them is, and rested the seventh day: wherefore IAUA blessed the Sabbath day and hallowed it." Exodus 20:8-11.

In the pope's encyclical calling for Sunday worship, he puffed up Sunday as "the Lord's day," but there's nothing in the Bible that says Sunday is "the Lord's day." Christ said He is "*Lord of the Sabbath*," Mark 2:27,28.

Some claim Sunday is the memorial to Christ's resurrection, but the Bible gives baptism by immersion as the memorial--

"We are buried with him by baptism into death: that like as Christ was raised up from the dead by the glory of the Father, even so we also should walk in newness of life," Romans 6:4.

Sunday not in Scripture

Sunday is not named anywhere in the Bible. It is

referred to eight times in the New Testament as the "first day" of the week. Six of those times were simply in connection with the resurrection when the women came to the tomb, etc, and in none are we told there would be a change in the day of worship.

Luke gives a good view of the sequence starting with the crucifixion on Friday--"*that day was the preparation, and the sabbath drew on. And the women also, which came with him from Galilee, followed after, and beheld the sepulchre, and how his body was laid. And they returned, and prepared spices and ointments; and rested the sabbath day according to the commandment: Now upon the first day of the week, very early in the morning, they came unto the sepulchre, bringing the spices.*" Luke 23:54-24:1.

In a dispute over Sabbath observance, Christ said he was "Lord of the Sabbath." As a good Jew, He kept the seventh day. The pope's encyclical with its references to edicts and tradition is NO authority for worshipping on the pagan day of sun worship, as much as the pope may want to appeal for everyone to honor the day that he blessed, as if he had the power to change the day when God says, "*I change not,*" Malachi 3:6.

Most Christians have the idea that the apostles honored Sunday. "Sunday" is not mentioned in the book of Acts. The "first day" of the week is mentioned only once when Paul had a Saturday night meeting and departed the next morning [Sunday]. But "Sabbath" is found nine times in Acts and twice it shows the apostle's custom to meet *"every Sabbath,"* Acts 15:21, 18:4.

The only other reference to "the first day" of the week is 1 Corinthians 16:2. "Upon the first day of the week let every one of you lay by him in store, as God has prospered him, that there be no gatherings when I come." Paul wanted to collect an offering for poor believers but he didn't want a last minute gathering of money when he arrived. Everyone was to do a weekly accounting at home. This does not support Sunday worship.

Origin of Christian Sunday Worship

"Sunday is a Catholic institution, and its claims to observance can be defended only on Catholic principles...From beginning to end of Scripture there is not a single passage that warrants the transfer of weekly public worship from the last day of the week to the first." *Catholic Press*, Sidney, Australia, August, 1900.

The Roman Emperor, Constantine, was a sun-worshiper and made a decree in 321 AD to honor Sunday. The pope, seeking his favor, blessed the Edict of Constantine.

"Question: Have you any other way of proving that the [Catholic] Church has power to institute festivals of precept, to command holy days?"

"Answer: Had she not such power, she could not have done that in which all modern religionists agree with her: She could not have substituted the observance of Sunday, the first day of the week for the observance of Saturday, the seventh day, <u>a change for which there is no Scriptural authority</u>." Stephan Keenan, *A Doctrinal Catechism*, pg 176

<u>"Restore All Things"</u>

It is our privilege to be "the Repairers of the Breach" in the law of God made by the papacy. We may share in the commission of Elijah *"to restore all things,"* Matthew 17:11.

There is more to this issue than the 7th day Sabbath. In Leviticus 23 there were seven annual holy convocations designed by God to teach us truths in His plan of salvation. "The Catholic Church abolished not only the Sabbath, but all the other Jewish festivals."

T. Enright, St. Alphonsus' Church, St. Louis, Mo.

The Yearly Sabbaths

Just as the Sabbath is a memorial of creation, Passover is a memorial to the greatest events of both Old and New Testament, the liberation from physical bondage in Egypt and the greater freedom from spiritual bondage and gift of eternal life that came with Christ's death for us at Passover.

1. "In the 14th day of the first month [the month begins with the first new moon after the equinox--a thin crescent in the western sky after sunset] is the Lord's Passover," Leviticus 23:5. Christ said, "Till heaven and earth pass, one yod or one tittle shall in no wise pass from the law, till all be fulfilled," Matthew 5:18. Christ fulfilled the *sacrificial part* by dying as the Passover lamb. We don't need to sacrifice animals, but the appointed times are still applicable.

2. Paul writes, *"Christ our Passover is sacrificed for us: Therefore let us keep the feast...with the unleavened bread of sincerity and truth,"* 1 Corinthians 5:7,8. He was referring to the Feast of Unleavened Bread. Leaven or yeast was a symbol of sin or corruption. Unleavened bread represented uncorrupted truth as embodied in the life and teachings of the Messiah. In a spiritual sense, this information is unleavened bread—uncorrupted truth that seeks restoration of IAUA's annual holy days. The first and 7th days of unleavened bread were "holy convocations."

3. Paul said not to let anyone judge us for keeping those holy days; they are a *"shadow of things to come,"* Colossians 2:16,17. If they are a shadow of things to come, they are not yet fulfilled [filled full].

4. The Hebrew word for "convocation" in Leviticus 23 is *mikvah.* It also means "rehearsal." We rehearse it in order to understand its meaning for when it may apply to us—they are *"a shadow of things to come."*

5. Paul said, *"Follow me as I follow Christ,"* 1 Corinthians 11:1. Paul observed Passover—"days of unleavened

bread" in Acts 20:6, Pentecost in Acts 20:16, and the Day of Atonement, Acts 27:9.

6. History shows that judgment fell at Passover on rejecters of truth for their time: Sodomites, Egyptians and Jews in 70 AD; the Flood came at the time of second Passover. History repeats, Ecclesiastes 3:15. *"All these things happened unto them for ensamples [types] and they were written for our admonition upon whom the ends of the world are come,"* 1 Corinthians 10:11. In a time of judgment, it would be well for us to meet as Christ asked the disciples to pray with Him, that judgment <u>pass over</u> us.

Pentecost

The first Pentecost was at Mt. Sinai--it was the giving of the law written on stone. After Christ ascended to heaven, Pentecost signaled His coronation and this time the law was written on the minds of His followers. We should keep Pentecost, praying His law will be written on our hearts as Ezekiel 36:25-27 suggests.

To this writer, Pentecost seems like a grid to screen out all false calendars. Currently the world mostly observes the Gregorian (papal) Calendar that does not recognize the new moon as the beginning of a new month. Centuries of this false system has even the Jews keeping Sabbath every Saturday (day of Saturn) when in Bible times, the 7th day Sabbath was counted from the new moon as we will see....

In Leviticus 23:6-**11** where the 15th day of the <u>1st month</u> was not only Passover, but it's a Sabbath, *shabbat* refers to the 7th day or 7th year everywhere else in Scripture. This is why it was called a "*high day*" in John 19:31 when Passover (annual Sabbath) and 7th-day Sabbath coincided at Christ's crucifixion.

Since that shows the 15th was a 7th-day Sabbath, it means they were counting *<u>from</u>* the New Moon and nowhere can we find a 7th-day Sabbath occurring on any day but the 8th, 15th, 22nd or 29th of the month.

This is also seen when we come to the 2nd month, we find the same numbers apply. On the 15th day, (Sabbath) God told Moses that He would send manna for six days but none on the 7th-day, it was "Sabbath." Exodus 16:1,4,5,22,23. This is the 1st use of the word Sabbath in the Bible when it occurred on the 22nd day of the 2nd month.

With TWO months in a row having Sabbath on the 15th and 22nd, they had to be counting from the New Moon and NOT a series of unending 7's as the Gregorian (Catholic) Calendar does, with the months having no relationship to the moon.

Pentecost is counted "*from the morrow after the Sabbath, from [the wave sheaf day which was the day Christ arose] seven __complete__ Sabbaths, even unto the morrow after the 7th Sabbath shall you number 50 days.*" Leviticus 23:15,16.

Why does it say "complete weeks"? Because the moon has a 29.5 day cycle. We don't count the New Moon Day because it does not have a complete week preceding it--it's an extra, uncounted day. Study the following graph with the NM as the New Moon Day...

The count to Pentecost begins on "the morrow (16th) after the Sabbath" on the 15th

16	17	18	19	20	21	22
23	24	25	26	27	28	29

[After 2 complete weeks with Sabbaths on the 22nd and 29th, there's a new moon day, but it's not part of a complete week; so it's not counted]

NM

2	3	4	5	6	7	8
9	10	11	12	13	14	15
16	17	18	19	20	21	22
23	24	25	26	27	28	29

30 (alternate month have 30 days because the lunar cycle is 29.5 but 30 isn't counted, because it's not part of a complete week, nor is the next New Moon Day. So far we have six complete weeks and Sabbaths above, counting from the wave sheaf day (16th). One more week: NM

2	3	4	5	6	7	8

P = Pentecost is the 50th day--

Here is an excellent short video explaining this calendar, https://www.youtube.com/watch?v=WxmKC_69MQY&ab_channel=TruthDefender I'm sorry you have to type, but it's worth the trouble!

Pentecost is the 9th day of the 2nd month after Passover is observed, "the morrow after the 7th Sabbath" when not counting incomplete weeks when there's an extra (30th) day nor does the New Moon Day count toward "seven Sabbaths complete."

This is different; but it's the only way to count "*from the morrow after the Sabbath*, [from the wave sheaf day which was the day Christ arose] *seven **complete** Sabbaths, even unto the morrow after the 7th Sabbath shall you number 50 days.*" Leviticus 23:15,16.

And it is also the only way to arrive at the 9th month, 24th day, a date seen THREE times in Haggai 2:10,18,21.

We arrives at that date with a reapplication of the 70 week prophecy in Daniel 9:24,25 that point to Messiah in the 69th week, but this is about our anointing as seen in Rev 11:3-6 with Elijah power to shut the heavens for 1260 days, that start on Pentecost that is counted from when the Flood began because the Flood had Passover timing, but in the 2nd month as seen in Genesis 7:1,4,11.

The basis of understanding Haggai's date is when the 3rd temple foundation is laid, but it's NOT built by Jews who want to kill lambs and ignore their Messiah who was the Lamb in Isaiah 53.

The 3rd Temple is us—"You are the temple," 1Cor 3:16 counting from Pentecost which gives Elijah power to shut the heavens, counting from the morrow after the Sabbath in the 2nd spring month (Numbers 9:10,11) as the days of Noe, but since there is Messiah (anointing) 69 weeks from a decree to rebuild Jerusalem after destruction by Muslims & the earthquake when the Lord shall roar from Jerusalem, the decree to rebuild the 3rd temple (living temple, us) goes 69 weeks to a 2nd anointing as Elisha got a double portion of Elijah's power and it comes the 69th week before 70 weeks end as seen in Haggai 2:10,18,20.

And the lunar calendar explained above is the only way to arrive at that date in Haggai, counting from 2nd Passover of Numbers 9:10,11 when the Flood began on the 17th day of the 2nd month. Count to Pentecost on the 9th day of the 4th month and that starts the 70 weeks, but don't forget to add the two days extra days as Passover begins on the 15th day, but the Flood began on the 17th day. The extra 2 days take us to the 24th day instead of the 22nd when the 3rd Sabbath of any month ends the week.

Admittedly, this is not an easy thing to see or count until one become acquainted with the lunar calendar, but then a year is 12 months of 30 days each, 360 days per year and we may find it's exactly 360 years for the earth to circle the sun after God shakes the heavens and earth,

Hag 2:6,7.

So from Pentecost to Pentecost will be 48 weeks in the 4th month, 8th day. This leaves 21 weeks to Messiah in the 69th week of Daniel 9 (our anointing) at the beginning of the 69th week that begins on the 15th day of the 9th month. That 69th week ends on the 22nd day (as the lunar calendar always has sabbaths on the 8th, 15th and 22nd of a month. The 70th week of Daniel 9's re-application begins on the 23rd day of the 9th month, and remember that the Flood came 2 days after Passover began, so the 2nd day after the Sabbath on the 24th corresponds to when the Flood began and it is the 70th week when the foundation of the 3rd temple (us) is laid. May God bless you as you try to understand this new concept which is not easy, but I can see no other way to get to the 9th month, 24th day when we, the 3rd temple have our foundation laid with a 2nd anointing like Elisha got.

Elisha was a type of Christ and he did every type of

miracle that Christ die, healing, raising a dead child, feeding a multitude, cleansing a leper, etc. May it be so for us...

The Sanctuary Service: a Model of the Plan of Salvation.

It was given "*according to all that I* [God] *show thee* [Moses] *after the pattern of the tabernacle*," Exodus 25:9. The pattern was in heaven where John later saw the candlesticks, altar and ark, Revelation 1:20; 8:3; 11:19.

- **Justification** by faith is illustrated by the slain lamb in the **outer court**. When we ask God to forgive our sin because Christ died in our behalf, bearing our sin, God forgives us. When we believe this, we are grateful, and this attitude of gratitude is the heart response that wants to serve Him and be worthy of His love. This is how we are justified [made right]. If we don't truly believe it all, we are not truly changed.
- **Sanctification** is represented by the bread in the

Holy Place. The Word of God is like bread, Matthew 4:4, the incense represented the prayers ascending to God, and the candlesticks represented our light that shines as we walk in the illumination of the Spirit that God gives us. This is a process of a lifetime and results in godliness or God-likeness so we will not be a misfit in heaven.

- **Perfection** of character is the experience of the **Most Holy Place** with the blotting out of sin (Acts 3:19) that has been previously confessed, 1 John 1:9. This occurred each year on the Day of At-one-ment. It typified Judgment Day and was kept with fasting and heart searching, but it was signaled 10 days earlier by—

The Feast of Trumpets

"*In the seventh month, in the first day of the month, shall ye have a sabbath, a memorial of blowing of trumpets, an holy convocation.*" This was to signal the Day of Atonement 10 days later. It gave opportunity to get right with God and fellowman. Because Judgment was executed at Passover (Exodus 12:12) it is reasonable to believe that the trumpet plagues in Revelation 8,9 may occur at the time of the symbolic service—the Feast of Trumpets, and sound yearly (one trumpet each year for six years with the 7th year having the 7 last plagues of Revelation 16).

This is like the conquest of Jericho when there was one trip with trumpets each day for six days and 7 trips on the 7th day, Joshua 6:4.

After the earthquake of Revelation 8:5, the 1st trumpet of Revelation 8:7 may bring economic collapse (when "all green grass was burnt up" because "as the flower of the grass, so shall the rich man fade," James 1:9-11, KJV).

Other timely fulfillments suggest our name will come up for Judgment on a Day of Atonement, the 10th day of the 7th month. *"Whatsoever soul it be that shall not be afflicted* [by fasting, Acts 27:9] *in that same day, he shall be cut off,"* Leviticus 23:29.

Judgment Day

Zechariah's vision of Joshua and the Angel applies with force in the closing up of God's account with individual Christians. Satan stands by to accuse, but the encouraging words are spoken, *"Take away the filthy garments...I have caused your iniquity to pass from you and I will clothe you with a change of raiment,"* Zechariah 3:1-10.

"Each one in the day of Judgment will stand in character as he really is; he will render an individual account to God. Every word uttered, every departure from integrity, every action that sullies the soul will be weighed in the balances of the sanctuary. Memory will be true and vivid in condemnation of the guilty one who in that day is found wanting. The mind will recall all the thoughts and acts of the past; the whole life will come in review like the scenes in a panorama. Thus everyone will be condemned or acquitted out of his own mouth and the righteousness of God will be vindicated." E.G. White, *Review & Herald*, 11-4-1884.

Feast of Tabernacles

The last annual Sabbaths begin after the day of atonement on the 15th day of the 7th month. *"The first day shall be a Sabbath, and on the eighth day shall be a Sabbath,"* Leviticus 23:39. They called it the Feast of Tabernacles, camping in booths made of palm branches in commemoration of the time their ancestors lived in the wilderness.

It was a time of spiritual instruction and blessing. *"In the last day, that great day of the feast, Christ stood and cried, saying, If any man thirst, let him come unto me, and drink. He that believes on me, as the scripture has said, out of his belly shall flow rivers of living water. But this spoke He of the Spirit, which they that believe on Him should receive."* John 7:37-39. We may expect this to be our experience one day soon!

These are the annual feast days that were changed by the papacy to pagan holidays having no biblical basis.

"He shall "think to change times and laws."

1.   We saw how this applied to the change of the 2nd Commandment that forbade the use of images. The catechism eliminated this commandment.

2.   Rome also changed the 7th day Sabbath to Sunday in the minds of countless Christians whose poor knowledge of Scripture allowed

the papacy to get away with it.

3.   Now we see the papacy changed the annual sabbaths to pagan holidays featuring witches, rabbits and reindeer. For example, could our Christmas tree custom be what is referred to here:

"Learn not the way of the heathen...For the customs of the people are vain: for one cuts a tree out of the forest, the work of the hands of the workman, with the ax. They deck it with silver and with gold; they fasten it with nails and with hammers, that it move not," Jeremiah 10:2-4.

Seven is the mark of end-time truth, and seven times God decries the breach in His statutes, judgments and sabbaths in Ezekiel 20:11-24. The word Sabbath includes both 7th day and annual Sabbaths. To divide the Word into some Sabbaths that we keep and some that we don't is a division of Christ, because He is "the

Word," John 1:1,14.

The annual Sabbaths are "holy convocations" and there are seven: the first and last day of unleavened bread associated with Passover, Pentecost, Feast of Trumpets, Day of Atonement, the first and last day of Tabernacles, Leviticus 23.

God said *"Remember the Sabbath day" because we are so prone to forget. He also said, "Remember ye the law of Moses...with the statutes* [which enjoined the annual Sabbaths] *and judgments. Behold I send you Elijah....Elijah shall truly come first and restore all things,"* Malachi 4:4,5, Matthew 17:11. It is our privilege to have a part in this restoration!

Poorly Translated Texts Explained:

1. Romans 14:5 sounds like it does not matter which day we keep, *"One man esteems one day above another:*

another esteems every day alike. Let every man be fully persuaded in his own mind." This is <u>not talking about worship</u>, but days for fasting or eating as the verses before and after it show. Worship is not mentioned in the chapter!

2. *"Let no man therefore judge you...in respect of an holy day, or of the new moon, or of the Sabbath days which are a shadow of <u>things to come</u>; but <u>the body</u> is <u>of Christ</u>,"* Colossians 2:16,17. This sounds like Christ is the substance and you can forget about the shadows. Translators added the word "<u>is</u>" and changed the meaning! It should read, *"Don't let anyone judge how you keep the holy days or new moons or Sabbaths [which are a shadow of things to come], but <u>the body of Christ</u>."* [The local church can judge *how* they will be kept.]

3. Oft-quoted as a reason not to observe annual sabbaths, Galatians 4:10 condemns a hair-splitting observance of the law's minutest details *in order to earn salvation.*

4. The council at Jerusalem, thought by many to have voided the need to observe these Sabbaths, did not require them *before baptism*. The reason was, "for Moses of old time has in every city them that preach him, being read in the synagogues every Sabbath day," Acts 15:21.

Failure to read the Old Testament and a misunderstanding of some New Testament texts due to translators having a Catholic perspective, has led to our misunderstanding on these points.

Origin of Easter

Eusebius, an early historian, stood for the Sabbath and the Passover at the Council of Nicea in 325 AD. He defended the Sabbath and named many martyrs, stating that "all of these kept the 14th of the month as the beginning of the Paschal festival in accordance with the Gospel." *The History of the Christian Church,* p 231. He was unable to prevail against Rome that wanted Sunday, rather than the 14th day of the month for Easter, a word that has more in common with the estrous cycle, fertility, eggs and rabbits than with Passover.

Paul shows that the memorial of Christ's death, burial and resurrection is not Easter, but baptism:

"We are buried with him by baptism into death: that like as Christ was raised up from the dead by the glory of the Father, even so we also should walk in newness of life," Romans 6:4. But this only works if baptism is by immersion—how can sprinkling bury anyone! In accepting sprinkling for baptism, Rome no longer had a resurrection symbol so it created "Easter" as a memorial to the resurrection.

Easter is a mistranslation in Acts 12:4 from the Greek word *"pascha"* which refers to Passover. *Catholic* means "universal" and in developing a church that has worldwide appeal, pagan symbols of life, regeneration and fertility, were "christianized."

New Moons

God told Moses that the new moon was the beginning of the month, with the *chodesh* (thin crescent) as the sign after the night of conjunction when no moon can be seen. But the calendar by Pope Gregory changed more than that. We now have month with no correlation to the holy time of the New Moon that we will celebrate in heaven, Isa 66:23.

Papal changes also mean the Sabbath was no longer the 7th day from the new moon which is no longer the start of the new month. Sunday is a never-ending series of 7's. Jews went with the change, observing Saturday every 7, but in Bible times, Sabbath was every 7th day from the new moon, falling on the 8th, 15th, 22nd and 29th of a month.

This author has offered $100 to anyone who can show a 7th day Sabbath on any day other than 8th, 15th, 22nd or 29.

Bible examples show Sabbath as on the 15th and 22nd when God was talking Moses on the 15th and He said there would be manna daily, but none on the 7th day that was Sabbath, Exod 16, and verse 23 is the first use of the word "Sabbath."

Another example is Christ's being in the grave on the 1st day of Passover. It was a high day (John 19:31) because the Passover's annual Sabbath coincided with the 7th day Sabbath.

It also means that Christ died and was put in the grave on what we call Friday afternoon, and rose early the first day. This is because God would not suffer His Holy One to see corruption, Ps 16:10; Acts 2:27.

This goes against Sabbath every 7 days from Creation as the Jews now celebrate Passover on Monday (April, 2024) . If

Christ were to wait till Sunday morning, as Martha told Christ when He was going to resurrect Lazarus, "It's been four days...he stinks". This is strong evidence against every 7 days for then Passover and the 7th day Sabbath would only coincide once in 7 years.

An understanding of God's calendar is represented by a pure woman, clothed in light and standing on the moon in Rev 12:1—it implies that she has a lunar understanding of God's appointed times in Leviticus 23 where *mo'ed* means appointed times.

They are designed to show that at the appointed time, One would come to whom the ceremony pointed, like Christ dying as the Passover Lamb on Passover. In like manner, events related to the 2nd coming must be similarly as the wedding parables blend an impending time of judgment.

We serve a loving God who made wise provision for us. We can look forward to when His kingdom is established and "from one new moon to another and from one Sabbath to another, shall all flesh come to worship before me, says IAUA," Isaiah 66:23. This prophecy reflects God's will. Any changes brought by man since then were not intended by God; He says, "*I am IAUA, I change not,*" Malachi 3:6.

An Interesting Catholic Statement

"When the time comes and men realize that the social edifice must be rebuilt according to eternal standards, be it tomorrow, or be it centuries from now, the Catholics will arrange things to suit said standards. [Like their standard for baptism, Easter, Halloween, Sunday, "Father," etc?]

Undeterred by those who prefer to abide in death, they will re-establish certain laws of life. They will restore Jesus to His place on high, and He shall no longer be insulted. They will raise their children to know God and to honor their parents. They will uphold the indissolubility of marriage, and if this fails to meet with approval of the dissenters, it will not fail to meet with the approval of their children. <u>They will make obligatory the religious observance of Sunday</u> on behalf of the whole of society and for its own good, revoking the permit for freethinkers and Jews to celebrate incognito, Monday or Saturday on their own account. Those whom this may annoy, will have to put up with the annoyance. Respect will not be refused to the Creator nor repose denied to the creature simply for the sake of humoring certain maniacs, whose frenetic condition causes them stupidly and insolently to block the will of a whole people." *The Liberal Illusion,* Louis Veuillot, published by the National Catholic Welfare Conference, Washington, DC.

"The doctrine which, from the very first origin of religious dissension, has been held by all bigots of all sects, when condensed into a few words, and stripped of rhetorical disguise, is simply this: I am in the right, and you are in the wrong. When you are the stronger, you ought to tolerate me; for it is your duty to tolerate truth. But when I am the stronger, I shall persecute you; for it is my duty to persecute error." Lord Macaulay, *"Essay on Sir James Mackintosh"* in *Critical and Historical Essays*.

Christ's Warning

"When you shall see the abomination of desolation, spoken of by Daniel the prophet, <u>standing where it ought not</u>, (let him that reads understand,) then let them that be in Judea flee to the mountains," Mark 13:14.

The early disciples understood His reference to Rome, and when Cestius, a Roman General came in 66 AD, Christians fled the city and were spared the siege by Titus in 70 AD.

Nearly 2000 passed when Pope John Paul II stood where he ought not—in Jerusalem. We are flirting with end-times.

What does it mean to be "in Judea"? That was the

area surrounding Jerusalem, *the center of true worship* in Christ's time. Papal history reveals a hatred that will persecute and martyr those who don't bow to her authority. Rome boasts the authority to change God's law, instituting Sunday instead Sabbath, and claiming Protestant homage in their observance of this day that has no biblical authority. The Jews experienced Rome's hatred in the holocaust. The pope signed a concordat blessing Hitler as a "favored son of the papacy." The document provided that all counties conquered would become Catholic. *"Let them that be in "Judea" flee to the mountains,"* Mark 13:14, Matt 24:15.

If the Sabbath was only for the Jews, why did Christ warn His disciples who would be Christians, *"pray that your flight be not in the winter, neither on the Sabbath day,"* Matthew 24:20. Those who value their freedom of worship need to consider Christ's warning to flee. This information suggests that we have seen the representative of the abomination that makes desolate, standing where [he] ought not.

"Sola Scriptura?"

As surely as the devil is in the details, there will be a Sunday law in the New World Order. It will come to the point where "*no man might buy or sell, save he that had the mark, or the name of the beast,*" Revelation 13:17. True Protestants whose motto is "Sola Scriptura," (only Scripture), will understand what's happening and will not go along with the New World Order.

Laodicea, the last lukewarm church, is said to be blind, Revelation 3:17. Christ's "knock" is an earthquake that brings us to an end of denominationalism and materialism. It focuses us on the fact that we are surrounded by systems that are failing, and we need to make a change. "*Babylon is fallen...come out of her, My people...*" Will we have the "guts" to do as Luther did when he stood alone? Or have we slid so far down that we are too weak to contend in matters of truth and freedom?

Summary

The papacy is well-described in Revelation 17, and also in Daniel 7:25 as the "little horn" that changed God's laws and persecuted the saints. Changes included sprinkling instead of immersion for baptism, elimination of the 2nd commandment forbidding images, splitting the 10th commandment to maintain 10, and changing the observance of the Sabbath to Sunday and the annual Sabbaths to paganized holidays like Halloween/All-saints Day, Easter, Valentine's Day and Christ mass.

It is our privilege to be "repairers of the breach" that the papacy has made in the law of God. In so doing, we are sharing in the work of Elijah who, before Christ returns, "must first come and restore all things." Because sun worship is so central to paganism, and because the papacy will be so central to the New World Order, this will be a coming battle for the few who are willing and brave enough to stand as the three Hebrews before the image of Babylon.

New World Order will be worse than the tyranny of the Old World when so many fled to America. "The Godfathers," offers excellent insights from Alberto Rivera, a former Jesuit, whose plain testimony cost him his life. "The Godfathers" is available in many Christian bookstores or from Chick Publications, PO Box 662, Chino CA 91706 or read online at http://www.chick.com/reading/comics/0114/0114_allinone.asp

The 5th Seal—"Martyrs for Christ"

"When He had opened the fifth seal, I saw under the altar the souls of them that were slain for the word of God, and for the testimony which they held: And they cried with a loud voice, saying, How long, O Lord"
Revelation 6:9,10.

This topic is also about Christ's name. HalleluIA is an international word meaning praise to God in every language. This sets the mood for the 5th Seal, https://www.youtube.com/watch?v=d_psFfD9Ib4&w=560&h=315

Outline

1. Apologetic for Jewish people.

2. Christ's name means salvation; it was changed.

3. The Name that Antichrist Will Personate.

4. Supporting clues from the book of Acts.

5. Hatred and opposition for the Savior's true name.

6. Questions and Discussion.

7.   The Name, the crown and 7 blessings.

8.   Whole-hearted; Contrasted signs of the covenant.

Overview

"*Hear, O Israel: The LORD our God is one LORD*" (Deut 6:4). On the surface, this seems against more than one. But the word for "one" is *echad*; it means a combined unity as when the evening and morning became one day, and when a man "*shall cleave unto his wife and they shall be one flesh*," Genesis 2:24. In the same way, the Godhead are *echad*—a combined unity of divine beings who are one in character, purpose, all-knowing, and all powerful. This combined unity fits the Hebrew word for God, *elohim,* used 2605 times in the Bible, because "elohim" is the *plural* form of the word for God. "*And God said, Let us make man in our image*," Genesis 1:26. Please allow the possibility that Abraham, father of the faithful, was a type of our heavenly Father. Abraham was tested on the point of willingness to give his son and amazingly responded, "*My son, God will provide Himself a lamb*." Genesis 22:8. If we don't allow for this, we cannot understand the sacrificial role of the Messiah's first advent described in Isaiah 53—

"**He is despised and rejected of men**; a man of sorrows, and acquainted with grief: and we hid as it were our faces from him; he was despised, and we esteemed him not. Surely he has borne our griefs, and carried our sorrows: yet we did esteem him stricken, smitten of God, and afflicted. But he was wounded for our transgressions, he was bruised for our iniquities: the chastisement of our peace was upon him; and with his stripes we are healed. All we like sheep have gone astray; we have turned every one to his own way; and the LORD hath laid on him the iniquity of us all," Isaiah 53:3-6.

The name of God's Son and the antichrist, the impostor, who will impersonate Him will be considered here. The fifth seal is about "*them that were slain for the word of God.*" John 1:1,14 shows that Christ was the Word made flesh and 7 times in the gospels we find references about our being hated for His name.

Martyrs will be specially honored in heaven. God is fair, and He will "*give* [reward] *to every man according as his work shall be*," Revelation 22:12. It will be a privilege to die for Him who died for us. This chapter suggests a surprise reason for end-time martyrdom—
the *Hebrew* name of Christ which has been effaced.

"What is His name and what is His Son's name, *if you can tell?*" Proverbs 30:4. Solomon's wonder suggests it is possibly something hidden. Shouldn't we also want to know?

A major clue is found in John 5:43—"*I am come in my Father's name and you receive me not. If another shall come in his own name, him you will receive.*"

If the Father's name was Zeus, they say it right in Italy when they pronounce the Savior's name "Yea Zeus!" In Latin America, it is "Hey Zeus!" In America, "Gee Zus!"

But Zeus was the savior god of Greek mythology who saved everyone and with no need of repentance. This may be a key to why "Jesus" is so popular, even among rock stars. There is a false belief that somehow, Jesus (like Zeus) is going to save everyone, even without repentance. This is a myth.

The broad way leads to destruction. Matthew 7:13. The times of this ignorance, God has winked at, but in a time of judgment, we must repent and go by the best information that we know. Acts 17:30,31.

1. Christ's Name Means Salvation

"*There is none other name under heaven given among men, whereby we must be saved*," Acts 4:12. It is more than the name of the One who saves. IAUshua means IAUA [the Godhead], saves. "Shua" means salvation. The KJV margins of Acts 7:45 and Hebrews 4:8 both show that Christ and Joshua had the same name. An Interlinear Translation shows the Greek word used for "Jesus" is the same word as for "Joshua."

A quick look implies Joshua and Jesus are equivalent, but they are far from equal! Original Bible names have been changed, and Joshua is closer to the Savior's Hebrew name, except **neither Hebrew nor Greek had the J letter or J sound.**

Yahshua is how Messianic Jewish Christians pronounce Christ's name. It uses the short, poetic form, *Yah,* from Psalm 68:4 and *shua* which means salvation in Hebrew. *Yahshua* means "Yah saves."

Equidistant Lettering Sequences [ELS] encode "Yahshua" in dozens of Messianic prophecies. In Isaiah 53 where Christ "is brought as a lamb to the slaughter and...taken from prison and from judgment," two verses later "he shall prolong his days" beginning with the 2nd yod, every 20 letters spells Yahshua Shmi—Yahshua is my name.(*Yeshua,* Yacov Rambsel, Frontier Research Publ)

For that to occur by random chance in this Messianic prophecy of Isaiah has been calculated as only one in 50 quadrillion!

One more example: From the 1st yod in the 1st word of the Bible, ["*In the beginning, God created the heavens and the earth*" Genesis 1:1] counting every 521 letters spells "Yahshua yakhol" which means, "He is able" or has the power!

2. Christ's Name Was Changed. The changes are explainable:

1.   Greek words ending in "a" are feminine, so the last "a" in Yahshua was changed to "s."

2.   Greek also had no equivalent to "sh" so "shua" became "sus" or "sous."

3.   The J replaced the Y sometime after the 1611 King James Version was first published. Early editions had His name spelled "Iesous."

Changing names violates custom and Scripture not to add or take away from it.

1.   Names–proper nouns–like "Bush" are not translated to mean shrub or little tree in other languages. They are transliterated to give the same sounds. Yet Bible names,

especially those with the yod [1st letter of God's name and Christ's name] were changed!

2.   The Savior said, "One yod...shall in no wise pass from the law until all be fulfilled," Matthew 5:18. His teaching was based on Deuteronomy 4:2—"*Ye shall not add unto the word that I command you, neither shall you diminish ought from it.*"

Young's Concordance shows "Joshua" begins with the Hebrew letters yod, hay, vav, the same three vowels as in God's name, IAUA [ee'-ah-oo"-ah], discussed in the 1st seal. Christ said, "*I am come in my Father's name,*" John 5:43. IAUshua [ee'-ah-oo-shoo"-ah] replaces the vowels eliminated by translators. They are the initials of the Godhead, IAU [ee-ah-oo] followed by shua[shoo-ah], which means salvation.

His name, IAUshua [ee-ah-oo-shoo-ah] means health or salvation in Hebrew. It also suggests the Godhead [IAUA] is the source of health and salvation. Besides being a beautiful, musical name, it carries the meaning of Their unity and involvement in our salvation. The first three Hebrew letters symbolize hand, light, and nail shown on the website http://God'sname1stSeal.wordpress.com There is no other name that has this meaning, and He said He will not give His name or glory to another, Isaiah 42:8.

"*You will be hated of all nations for My name,*" Christ said. His name was partly why IAUshua was rejected.

When Satan impersonates Christ, he will come in his own name [Zeus derivative]

"Him, whose coming is after the working of Satan with all power and signs and lying wonders, because they received not the love of the truth, [true name which means salvation] that they might be saved. And for this

cause God shall send them strong delusion, that they should believe a lie," 2 Thessalonians 2:9-11.

A strange thing happens to many who profess to love the Lord. He said He was "*the truth*" (John 14:6), but when some learn the truth about His name, they show preference for a lie. In doing so, we deny Him as Peter did, Matthew 26:72.

If we don't move in the direction of truth when we learn it, soon the lie does not seem so bad—we have all experienced doing something wrong because we did not take a positive stand early. When "*the son of perdition ...sits in the temple of God, showing himself that he is God*" (2 Thessalonians 2:3,4), the most identifying characteristic of antichrist will not be his looks or miracles, but his name! Satan cannot use Christ's true name. "*My name and my glory will I not give to another*," Isaiah 42:8.

Clues from the Book of Acts

1.   On the way to Damascus, Saul "heard a voice...in the Hebrew tongue...I am Jesus" This could not be— Hebrew had no "J" letter or sound. Translators changed His name, but couldn't hide the fact that He had a Hebrew name. I*esous* is a Greek name, Acts 24:14,15.

2.   "*A certain sorcerer, a false prophet, a Jew whose name was Barjesus...*[skip one verse] "*but Elymas the sorcerer (for so is his name by interpretation) withstood them.*" Acts 13:6-8. This says "Barjesus" means "sorcerer." "Bar" means son. "Son of Jezeus" means "by interpretation ...sorcerer." The point is that Zeus was linked to sorcery, the Savior had nothing to do with sorcery.

This also shows "Jesus" was a common Greek name then. Do we think the angel would have told Mary to give her Son [born into the tribe of Judah from David's lineage] a Greek name, a derivative of the Greek savior god Zeus?

Why would the Holy Spirit impress Luke to include this information in the book of Acts, unless it was an important clue? God knew Satan's intent to change Christ's name and He put these clues in Scripture to help us!

666

The numerology of "Christ Jesus" fits the warning of 666 in Revelation 13:18 when no one can buy or sell unless he or she has that number. The Greek letters Chi, Xi [pronounced ki and zi as in pie] and Sigma add up to 666. Their capitalized symbols are X = 600, Z = 60, and S = 6. Some dictionaries show X can mean Christ [as in Xmas]. So XZS, Christ ZeuS will be 666 when Satan personates Christ as the Savior in the temple at Jerusalem— someday soon!

This may be one reason why *"Many will say to me in that day, Lord, Lord, have we not prophesied in your name? Then will I profess unto them, I never knew you: depart from me,"* Matthew 7:22,23. The word, "know" is an intimate knowledge as when Joseph did not know Mary until after the Savior was born.

We seek a covenant with God that is like a spiritual marriage. We have not really known Him like we expect to in the end-time period. A bride must accept her husband's name. Are we open to receiving Him and His "new name," Rev 3:12? If so, we may be wed to Him spiritually.

Hatred for IAUshua

A 7-fold statement is God's "signature" on truth for the end-time. Below are seven statements that suggest we will be hated for the Savior's true name. Most Bibles say, "hated for my name's sake." "Sake" was added by translators in all texts except *Luke* 21:17. Here is how they should actually read.

1.   *"You shall be hated of all men for My name: but he that endures to the end shall be saved. But when they persecute you in this city, flee into another,"* Matthew 10:22,23.

2.   *"Then shall they deliver you up to be afflicted, and shall kill you: and you shall be hated of all nations for My name,"* Matthew 24:9.

3.   *"You shall be hated of all men for My name, but he that shall endure unto the end, the same shall be saved,"* Mark 13:13.

4.   *"Before all these, they shall lay their hands on you and persecute you, delivering you up to the synagogues*

and into prisons, being brought before kings and rulers for My name," Luke 21:12.

5.   "You shall be betrayed by parents and brethren and kinsfolk and friends; and some of you shall they cause to be put to death. And you shall be hated of all men for My name's sake," Luke 21:17.

6.   "The servant is not greater than his lord. If they have persecuted Me, they will also persecute you; if they have kept my saying, they will keep yours also. But all these things will they do unto you for My name, because they know not him that sent me," John 15:20:21.

7.   "I will show him how great things he must suffer for My name," Acts 9:16.

Adding "sake" tends to obscure His name as an issue. Some translations merely say we will be hated for His sake, not even mentioning His name. This is a shameful twist of truth.

Richard Baron, in his book, *I Was a New Age Priest*, tells how the name "Jesus" is increasingly used in the spirit world in connection with Christ as the Maitreya to come. It is also popular among rock music stars. Something doesn't fit. Yahshua said, "*You shall be hated of all nations for My name.*"

This proved true for His disciples who all suffered a martyr's death except John who typifies the 144,000, maybe for his willingness to identify with an unpopular Christ. When the other disciples had fled, John was with Christ at the cross and was later spared being a martyr.

He typifies the 144,000 who follow closely and have the Father's name and the Son's name, Rev 14:1, RSV. If we are willing to identify with an unpopular name, we may be "*brought before kings and rulers.*" This is part of "*restore all things,*" Matthew 17:11.

After a beating, the disciples rejoiced "that they were counted worthy to suffer shame for his name, Acts 5:41. Because IAUshua said this would be our experience, if we are not hated for His name, we must not have the right name!

Many Against His Name!

When asked about the end of the world, the first thing Christ said after being asked—"*Do not be deceived... many will come against My name,*" Matthew 24:5, Mark 13:6, Luke 21:8.

But *our* Bibles don't say "*against*" because that would be a clue to "name" problems and we would be quickly polarized on any name change. Translation has it "many will come *in* My name" and since we don't see many claiming to be "Jesus Christ," we are lulled into thinking all is well.

You can verify this in most libraries with an Interlinear Bible. In Matthew 24:7 where *"nation will rise <u>against</u> nation"* you can see the Greek word translated against is the same word translated "in"— "many will come in My name." Both texts should read against. Translators did the same thing in Mark 13:6, compare vs 8, and in Luke 21:8–compare vs 10.

Speaking of His second coming symbolized by His transfiguration, Christ said, "Elias truly shall first come, and restore all things," Matthew 17:11. "All things" includes the names! For further information on the pronunciation, the reader is referred to the chapter on God's covenant name—Christ said, "I am come in my Father's name," John 5:43.

Questions and Discussion

Most objections have already been dealt with in discussion of the Father's name. Here are a few additional considerations.

1. Doesn't Christ have many names?

He said, "*I am the bread of life...I am the light of the world...I am the good shepherd*." He is Lord–the Hebrew word is "adonai," but these are titles or appellations, not names.

2. Millions have prayed in the name of Jesus and had their prayers answered. "*The times of this ignorance God winked* at, [He honored those prayers] *but now commands all men everywhere to repent, because He has appointed a day in which He will judge the world,*" Acts 17:30,31. We are entering a judgment time when

we can no longer plead ignorance. We should go by the best information we have.

3. There are cultural variations in pronunciation. Why is exactness so important?

If we do the best we know, "God winks," In Bible times pronunciation was important:

When those Ephraimites which were escaped said, Let me go over; the men of Gilead said unto him, Art you an Ephraimite? If he said Nay; then they said to him, Say now Shibboleth: and he said Sibboleth, for he could not frame to pronounce it right. Then they took him, and slew him at the passages of Jordan: and there fell at that time of the Ephraimites 42,000," Judges 12:6. Note the "s" sound meant death while the "sh" sound meant life. You don't have to be a zoology major to know that serpents make the "s" sound. Occult books show "S" is

Satan's sign. Christ's true name ends in shua. It means "salvation" in Hebrew.

4. If His name is an issue, why didn't He say so in the message to the churches in Revelation? Maybe He did...

Christ's Name in the Churches

1. Ephesus: *"for my name* [sake is a supplied word] *hast labored,"* Revelation 2:3.

2. Smyrna: Died as faithful martyrs. Name not mentioned but preserved for next church period.

3. Pergamos: *"you hold fast my name,"* Revelation 2:13.

4. Thyatira: Unfaithful church with Jezebel who promoted false worship [Baal means "lord," God's name disappeared from Scripture, replaced by LORD or GOD in

all caps. Also, Iesous/Jesus introduced into Scripture. Dictionaries show *Jesuit* as "a member of the Society of Jesus." Will we be in that society? Christ said, *"Broad is the way that leads to destruction,"* Matthew 7:13. This is an appeal to everyone who may still prefer the familiar because it feels comfortable. We must go by the light of truth and make a change, even if we stand alone as Luther did.

5. Sardis: *"You have a Name that you live and are dead,"* Revelation 3:1. Protestant Reformers accepted Iesous from translators instead of protesting.

6. Philadelphia: *"Thou has not denied my name,"* Revelation 3:8. This was not an issue in their time. They lived up to the light they had. Overcomers will receive "*My new name*." It will be new to them in the resurrection, but Solomon says, *"There is no new thing under the sun."* It will seem new, but He who takes us to

the Promised Land in the end has the same name as he who took Israel across Jordan--IAUshua!

7. Laodicea: The "aggelos" [Greek word for messenger] is said to be blind with Christ knocking at the door. <u>A blind person must ask, Who is there?</u> <u>This focus is on His name</u> and we've been blind not to see this. We are told to <u>get eyesalve</u>—"*Thy name is as ointment,*" Song of Solomon 1:3. Furthermore, His name is as a fragrant ointment that is appealing for marital union—"*therefore do the virgins love Thee*!" Laodicea with no interest in His true name is nauseous, and will be spewed out, but individuals may choose His name.

The Bible Forbids "Jesus!"

Knowing His cunning adversary, God foresaw the change in names and expressly forbade using names of heathen deity. "*Make no mention of the name of other gods,*" Exodus 23:13. This forbids using "Zeus" or names derived from it, Jesus or "Hey Zeus" as they pronounce it in Spanish. If we pray the Lord's prayer, "*Thy kingdom come*," means we seek compliance with His plan.

Familiar songs make this difficult, but substituting "IA" [ee-ah, the short form of God's name] or "shua" [shoo-ah, meaning salvation] as an abbreviated form of IAUshua allows these songs. Doing so enables us to be obedient to Scripture and also to help "*restore all things*," Matthew 17:11.

A True Story

A wealthy man married late in life and though his wife was able to conceive, she died in childbirth. All the man had from the one he loved was condensed into a little boy that had a sweet disposition, but he wasn't quite right. Perhaps he had Down's Syndrome. The man loved his son and hired a nursemaid to take care of him who also loved the boy. But there was loneliness—the other boys wouldn't play with him because he was different.

His father hired an artist to paint a life-size portrait that was finished for his 12th birthday and the father bought a pony for him and invited other boys to come and enjoy the party. They poked fun at the portrait and the party didn't turn out as the kind father hoped. A tragedy ensued; the pony tripped, fell and rolled onto the little boy, killing him. The man, heart-broken with a loss of his wife and then his only son, died within the following year.

The auction of his estate brought people from all over England, eager to bid on paintings and items of value. The auctioneer, oddly enough, chose the portrait of the little boy to go first. But nobody would bid on it—probably because it was a little odd. Finally, in desperation, the auctioneer said, "Would anyone give even a shilling for this picture."

The little maid, who was so poor she didn't expect to buy anything, suddenly waved her handkerchief—"I have a shilling!" she said. "Sold" said the auction, who then addressed the crowd: "Ladies and gentlemen. This auction is over. The entire estate goes to the buyer of the little boy's portrait!"

The true pronunciation of the Savior's name may seem odd, like the boy, but the end will have poetic justice for those who love the truth. IAUshua said, "*I am the way, the truth and the life*," John 14:6. Scripture says He was "*as a root out of a dry ground, He has no form nor comeliness...that we should desire Him*," Isaiah 53:2. Christ purposed that money, power or fame would not be what attracted others to Him, only the beauty of heavenly truth. If we love Him, we will love His name, and like the auction story above, "*he that has the Son, has life*."

The Name and the Crown go together

We discuss now the 1st seal with the rider having a crown because it fits the story above and our Savior who wore the crown. We don't think of it because most artists paint Him as having a well-trimmed beard, but evidence suggests that He was a Nazirite. He came to fulfill the law that includes something unpleasant to our modern culture: *"You shall not round the corners of your heads, neither shall you mar the corners of your beard,"* Leviticus 19:27.

The Greek word for the crown is *stefanos;* "wreath." The hair and beard form a wreath for the face, and like the crown of thorns, it is painful—to our pride. The first mention of crown in Scripture is Genesis 49:26—

"the crown of the head of him [Joseph] *that was separate."* *Strong's Concordance* shows "separate" comes from nazir—"consecrated (as prince, a Nazirite)." Joseph let his hair and beard grow in prison until he went to Pharaoh, Genesis 41:14.

Elijah was "a hairy man" and a type of John the Baptist who was consecrated from birth. John was the forerunner for Christ's 1st advent; we are to prepare the way for His 2nd coming. Being a Nazirite was not restricted to men; women may also be Nazirites, Numbers 6:2.

Samson was a Nazirite and there are many parallels between him and Christ. An angel came with instruction before their births. Samson was the strongest man physically; Christ was the strongest man spiritually. Samson delivered Israel from the Philistines when he died; Christ delivered spiritual Israelites by His death.

The word "nazir" is linked to the covenant by 7 Nazirite blessings, seven being a sign of the covenant and end-time truth. *Strong's Concordance* for *shaba:* "to seven oneself, (as if by repeating a declaration seven times)...take an oath" or make a covenant.

7 Blessings on the Nazirites

1. *"The LORD bless you*

2. *and keep you,*

3. *The LORD make his face shine upon you,*

4. *and be gracious unto you:*

5. *The LORD lift up His countenance upon you*

6. *and give you peace.*

7. *And they shall put My name upon the children of Israel,"* Numbers 6:24-27.

Many people are familiar with the 1st six, but the 7th blessing should excite us! If we don't put God's name on anyone else but ourselves, it would be sufficient reward to be among those who have His name, Revelation 14:1. Look at #3 and #5. The meaning of *"lift up His countenance"* is [set, lay, put] His countenance [face—same Hebrew word as the previous verse] on those who separate themselves to Him by letting their hair and beard grow. This is what the chapter of Numbers 6 is all about.

We want God's name to seal and protect us in the end, but Numbers 6:25-27 links putting His name on us with *putting His face on us*! Since the chapter is about Nazirites who let their hair and beard grow, we might wonder, Can we have His name, if we do not want His face?

"Beloved, now are we the sons [and daughters] *of God, and it does not yet appear what we shall be: but we*

know that, when He shall appear, we shall be like Him...God created man in His own image," 1 John 3:2; Genesis 1:27. Parents appreciate their image or resemblance in their children. God will look to see His likeness in us.

Since Numbers 6:24-27 shows that putting God's name and His face on His people go together, this process is in the context of the white horse. Revelation 6:1-2 is called a "seal." John sees 144,000 sealed; they have the Father's name (Revelation 14:1) and also have His face!

Pros and Cons

If we are concerned for God's name and want to see it restored, if we sense Christ's concern for His Father's name and if we appreciate the 7-fold blessings we expect to receive, why should we not let our hair and beard grow as He has specified?

We may not see how letting our hair and beard grow will accomplish what it says, but that's God's problem! His word *"shall not return unto [Him] void but it shall accomplish what [He] please,"* Isaiah 55:11. He *"has chosen the foolish things of the world to confound the wise,"* 1 Corinthians 1:27.

Numbers 6:2-9

"When either man or woman shall separate themselves to vow a vow of a Nazarite, to separate themselves unto IAUA, He shall separate himself from wine and strong drink, and shall drink no vinegar of wine, or vinegar of strong drink, neither shall he drink any liquor of grapes, nor eat moist grapes, or dried...All the days of the vow of his separation there shall no razor come upon his head: until the days be fulfilled, in the which he separates himself unto IAUA, he shall be holy, and shall let the locks of the hair of his head grow. All the days that he separates himself unto IAUA he shall come at no dead

body. He shall not make himself unclean for his father, or for his mother, for his brother, or for his sister, when they die: because the consecration of his God is upon his head. All the days of his separation he is holy unto IAUA. And if any man die very suddenly by him, and he has defiled the head of his consecration; then he shall shave his head in the day of his cleansing, on the seventh day shall he shave it."

Some say Christ was not a Nazirite because He associated with those who ate and drank. There's no evidence or record that He tasted of the vine until the Last Supper in a choice to end His vow. He was going before Pilate (like Joseph who ended his vow and shaved before seeing Pharaoh.) Christ didn't shave; the Bible says He "*gave* [His] *cheeks to them that plucked off the hair*," Isaiah 50:6. Men know how painful it is to have even one hair plucked from their face, but to have the whole beard plucked must have caused raw bleeding and unimaginable pain. They probably did this to taunt

Him, because the law allowed polling [plucking of a hair] for a Nazirite.

"The things that are God's" may protect us

When Christ was asked about paying tax, He requested a coin and said, "Whose is this image and superscription?" They said Caesar's. He said, *"Render to Caesar the things that are Caesar's, and to God the things that are God's."* Like the coin, we bear God's image and are His, Genesis 1:26. Would we want to deface or mar that image? *"Render...to God the things that are God's,"* Mark 12:17.

Unless we are martyred, if we are riding the white horse of truth, we may expect protection from the red, black or pale horse [blood shed, famine, disease and death.] How being a Nazirite is protective is not obvious. Avoiding contact with dead body includes avoiding meat [which is a high risk for heart disease, cancer and some serious infectious diseases] or contact with a dead person. "*He shall not make himself unclean for his father or his mother...*" Numbers 6:7. This might save us from anthrax or bubonic plague later [the pale horse.] Further protection may result from our being ostracized from society by our woolly appearance and, therefore, protected from judgments that fall on unbelievers.

Being "Whole-Hearted"

Scripture says David was "*a man after* [God's] *own heart*," Acts 13:22. This is partly because David was "whole-hearted." Six times in Psalm 119 he uses that phrase. For example, "*Blessed are they that keep his testimonies, and that seek him with the whole heart.*" This links seeking Him with keeping His law, and the law enjoins our looking like a Nazirite, Leviticus 19:27.

If that isn't enough, the Rule of First Use provides further insight to being "whole-hearted." The Hebrew words *kol leb* [whole heart] are first used in Judges 16:17 where

Samson, after being badgered by Delilah, "told her all his heart, and said unto her, There has not come a razor upon mine head; for I have been a Nazarite." This context suggests being whole-hearted includes being a Nazirite.

A word of caution for those choosing to accept this token of the covenant: Numbers 6 specifies avoidance of grapes or vinegar. On more than one occasion, this writer has broken the vow, shaved bald and started over because it is easy to overlook grapes or raisins in a fruit salad, vinegar in the salad dressing, or a fruit juice blend that contains grape.

Christ said, "*This cup is the new testament in my blood: this do ye, as oft as ye drink it, in remembrance of me,*" 1 Corinthians 11:25. In so doing, He gave us a legitimate basis to shave—a fresh start each spring when we observe the tokens of His sacrifice at Passover. A fresh start also prevents men from having long hair as women

have, for that is a shame, according to Paul, 1
Corinthians 11:14,15.

Contrasting Signs of the Covenant

God covenanted to make Abraham a great nation and
give him the Promised Land. The name, Abraham, means
"father of a multitude." It must have been an
embarrassment to him—he had no children! Abraham
tried to fulfill this in his own way, taking Hagar as a wife.
God told him to quit trying and trust Him.

As a sign of the covenant, that he believed God would
make of him a great nation, (even when he was old and
had no children) God asked him to circumcise himself, a
token of amputation, as if to say, Even if I'm old,
childless and cut off, I believe God can make of me a
great nation as He said. Imagine the faith of Abraham to
do this at age 99, before the days of anesthesia, not only

to himself but all his servants. This sign of the covenant was a painful experience!

Could it be that IAUA is giving us an almost painless opportunity to make a covenant with Him that would honor His name and place His face upon us. It's painless except for our pride—"*Humble yourselves therefore under the mighty hand of God, that He may exalt you in due time,*" 1 Peter 5:6.

We live in an age of "politically correct" messages by politicians that can bend the truth to fit both sides. Here is a message that's not smooth or slick. It says, I'm most interested in pleasing God, not the press.

A public confession of end-time truth won't save us anymore than circumcision saved the Jews, but it is linked to God's seven-fold blessing, and maybe our pride needs humbling. Do we esteem the praise and opinions of others more than that of God? If we don't need the 7-fold blessing, maybe God doesn't need us.

"I gave my back to the smiters, and my cheeks to them that plucked off the hair," Isaiah 50:6. Those who love their Redeemer will rejoice at every opportunity to share with Him in humiliation, shame and reproach. Their love for IAUshua makes suffering for His sake sweet; and they know that if they suffer with Him, they shall also reign with Him.

This is not for those who are just trying to reach the lowest standard for heaven.

Note: We have two more topics to consider before we covenant to be His. In the meantime, if you do not want long hair in the summer, you might cut it short before you make the covenant. Then we would expect to let our hair grow until Passover in the spring when we partake of His emblems. The grape juice breaks the Nazirite vow on the eve of the Feast of Unleavened Bread, and "*he shall shave his head in the day of his cleansing, on the seventh day shall he shave it*," Numbers 6:9.

The 6th Seal—the Promised Land!

"*When He had opened the sixth seal, there was a great earthquake; and the sun became black as sackcloth of hair, and* the moon became as blood; And the stars of heaven fell unto the earth, even as a fig tree casts her untimely figs, when she is shaken of a mighty wind. And the heaven departed as a scroll when it is rolled together; and every mountain and island were moved out of their places. And the kings of the earth, and the great men, and the rich men, and the chief captains, and the mighty men, and every bond man, and every free man, hid themselves in the dens and in the rocks of the mountains; And said to the mountains and rocks, fall on us, and hide us from the face of Him that sits on the throne, and from the wrath of the Lamb: For the great day of His wrath is come; and who shall be able to stand?" Revelation 6:12-17.

Music: The National Anthem of Israel: Notice the words: http://www.youtube.com/watch?v=af6VgvkWq48

Outline

1.   The New Covenant is for spiritual Israel, end-time.

2.   Troubles for America; the Greek word for church, *ekklesia* means "called out."

3.   Two 3 ½ year periods for the church in the wilderness

4.   "Sell what you have" precedes the Promised Land.

5.   Summary

Overview

In the sixth seal, "*every mountain and island were moved out of their places.*" It parallels the time of the plagues, especially the

7th –"*every island fled away, and the mountains were not found,*" Revelation 16:20. For people living on islands, the following information should be good news! The sixth seal ends with many wanting to hide; they ask, "*Who shall be able to stand?*" Revelation 7 shows **those who are sealed are those who are able to stand.** That's why we are considering this information that is linked contextually to the seals. If we understand and commit ourselves to it by a covenant, we can stand in God's strength.

The sealing includes renewing a covenant with God, as in Nehemiah 9:38. We now look at **God's covenant to give the Promised Land to spiritual *Israel*. "*If you be Christ's, you are Abraham's seed and heirs according to the promise,*"** Galatians 3:29. Seven times God told Abraham He would give him that land. The New Covenant promise is not about a new or different covenant, but the promise (covenant) to write the laws of the covenant in our hearts:

"*I will put my spirit within you and cause you to walk in my statutes and ye shall keep my judgments and do them,*" Ezekiel 36:27. Jeremiah shows this has an end-time context:

"*Lo, the days come, says IAUA, that I will bring again the captivity of my people Israel and Judah, and **I will cause them to return to the land that I gave to their fathers, and they shall possess it**…for <u>I am with thee, says IAUA, to save thee: though I</u>*

*make a full end of all nations whither I have scattered thee, yet will I not make a full end of thee... **in the latter days** ye shall consider it,"* Jeremiah 30:3,11,24. This "latter day" gathering of God's people is the setting or context for the New Covenant promise to write His law in our hearts, Jeremiah 31:33.

Land = Wealth

The basis of true wealth in our world is land. That's why it's called *"real"* estate. Land can grow crops for food, and trees for houses and paper; land has minerals like iron, etc. But as the world gets more populated, there is not enough land for some people's greed.

God covenanted to give to Abraham the most valuable real estate in the world—*"from the river of Egypt to the great river, the river Euphrates,"* Genesis 15:18. This is an "unbelievable deal," except God is the giver and if we can believe His word, the real estate is for us, because *"If you are Christ's, you are Abraham's seed, and heirs according to the promise,"* Galatians 3:29.

Can God deliver the goods? The millions of Jews in that little area of Israel may wonder—that's why Rabin was assassinated—he was giving away land that God had given them. And now we have the U.S. trying to force Israel to divide their land with Palestinians.

The Covenant is for End-time

In Daniel 12:7, the man in linen swears. The Hebrew word *shaba* means he sevens himself, as in an oath or covenant. This suggests that when God says something *seven times*, it pertains to the covenant and to God's plan to accomplish in end-time what His ancient people failed to realize because of their lack of faith. Seven times God said He would give Abraham that land, Genesis 12:1,7; 13:15,17; 15:7,18; 17:8.

Do we have faith to trust the Bible, or do we prefer human reasoning and our own devices? The covenant can be *our covenant*; it truly is an option. It was a one-sided promise by God to Abraham who took animals, sacrificed and divided them, and should have passed between them as if to say, "May I be torn apart like this meat if I fail to keep my part."

But God caused a deep sleep to fall on Abraham, and only God, as a "burning lamp" went between the sacrifice—He alone has the obligation of the covenant, Genesis 15:9-18. The covenant is freely offered and we can take it or leave it. But **ignoring it is ignoring a provision for Abraham's seed when New World Order will force all into false worship**. The sternest warning in the Bible is against those who go along with NWO, Revelation 14:9,10.

Spiritual Israel

You may say, "That was for Abraham and his seed. I'm not Jewish." If you believe the Bible, and accept the Messiah, you don't need to be Jewish. It says, "*If you are Christ's, then you are Abraham's seed* [spiritually] *and heirs according to the promise,*" Galatians 3:29.

"About the time of the end, a body of men will be raised up who will turn their attention to the prophecies and insist upon their literal interpretation, in the midst of much clamor and opposition." *Sir Isaac Newton.*

It's amazing that men of intellect could see in the future what some of us can't see in the present. God is going to unite Jews who will accept IAUshua as their Messiah and Christians who will accept the torah as "*the law of IAUA [that] is perfect, converting the soul,*" Psalm 19:7. We see this foretold in Ezekiel 37 where the dry bones come together to become a body with flesh:

"*These bones are the house of Israel...I will...bring you into the land of Israel...neither shall they be divided into two kingdoms any more at all,*" Ezekiel 37:11,12,32.

"Church" Means Called Out

The meaning of church [the Greek word, *ekklesia,* means "called-out"] in the end-time must be more than at any other "calling-out" in history. And to mean more, it must be more than an ideological calling out of "Babylon" when we are still surrounded by Babylon. Here's the last prophetic call in the Bible:

"*Babylon the great is fallen....Come out of her, my people, that ye be not partakers of her sins, and that ye receive not of her plagues,*" Revelation 18:2,4.

There will be a prophetic opportunity to leave America, probably as a courtesy from the U.S. Government—with the "*wings of a great eagle*," Revelation 12:14. This may be God's way of protecting us, just as He provided for Jews to return to their land from Persia at Artaxerxes' decree in 457 BC. Those who did not return faced death in the days of Queen Esther.

"*All these things happened to them for examples ...written for our admonition on whom the ends of the world are come,*" 1 Corinthians 10:11. Going to the Promised Land will require major faith; but staying to face the New World Order is presumptuous and risks the wrath of God. [Revelation 14:9,10]. "That which God purposed to do for the world through Israel, the chosen nation, He will finally accomplish through His church on earth today...even to His covenant-keeping people...and to them will be fulfilled all the covenant promises made by [IAUA] to His ancient people," Ellen White, *The Captivity & Restoration of Israel,* 713,714, a book the publishers renamed as "Prophets and Kings." Ellen White's title, taken from Jeremiah 30:3.

This may be an unpopular message, but even though God be with us, bring a weapon!

"*Moses said unto them, If ye will do this thing, if ye will go armed before IAUA to war, And will go all of you armed over Jordan before IAUA, until he has driven out his enemies from before him,*" *and the land be subdued before IAUA: then afterward ye shall*

return, and be guiltless before IAUA, and before Israel; and this

land shall be your possession before IAUA. But if ye will not do so,

behold, ye have sinned against IAUA: and be sure your sin will

find you out,"

Numbers 32:20-23.

Depending on His Promises

IAUA has a plan to save us from the wine of His wrath when the

mark is forced on everyone. When Israel came out of Egypt, they

faced giants. Now the giants have tanks. At this point, IAUA

becomes responsible for His people as a movement:

"I will bring you into the wilderness of the people, and there will I

plead with you face to face, like as I pleaded with your fathers in

the wilderness of the land of Egypt, so will I plead with you, says

IAUA. And I will cause you to pass under the rod and I will bring

you into the bond of the covenant and I will purge out from

among you the rebels," Ezekiel 20:35,36.

May the evil heart of unbelief be purged out of us so we are not

purged out.

The 144,000 sing the song of Moses and the Lamb. Moses' song

ends with the promise that IAUA *"will be merciful unto His land*

and to His people," Deuteronomy 32:44. The margin refers to

Psalm 85:1—*"IAUA, you have been favorable unto Your land; You*

have brought back the captivity of Jacob."

The song of the Lamb may be Psalm 23: "*IAUA is my shepherd...He leads me in the pathways of righteousness for His name sake...Yea though I walk through the valley of the shadow of death, I will fear no evil...*"

"*As a shepherd seeks out his flock in the day that he is among his sheep that are scattered; so will I seek out my sheep and will deliver them out of all places where they have been scattered...I will bring them...to their own land and feed them on the mountains of Israel,*" Ezekiel 34:12,13.

Being Where the Action Is

Antichrist [meaning, in place of Christ to personate Him] will come and seek to draw everyone to himself. We described this in the fifth seal, "*so that he as God sits in the temple of God, showing himself that he is God,*" 2 Thessalonians 2:4.

It will be like the golden image on the plain of Dura when everyone bowed except Shadrach, Meshach and Abednego. They were thrown into the fiery furnace, and then were brought out when the king saw *"one like the Son of God"* with them in the furnace. Daniel 3 was written for us when the New World Order [the image beast of the papal Old World Order, Rev 13:14] requires worship or death. Those who die as martyrs will receive their reward in the resurrection, but some are spared.

Two 3 ½ Year Periods

"*The woman* [church] *fled into the wilderness where she had a place prepared of God...1260 days,"* Revelation 12:6.

• In history, there were 1260 years of the Holy Roman Empire from 538 to 1798 when Napoleon took the pope prisoner, and he died in exile. The 1260 days of Revelation 11:3 were *"each day for a year"* in prophecy, Numbers 14:34 and Ezekiel 4:6.

• In the end-time, these are literal days: 1260 days = 3 ½ years for the New World Order when the devil has "great wrath, because he knows that he has but a *short time,"* Revelation 12:12. "Short time" actually refers to the end-time period of seven years that have *two* 3 ½ year periods—

1. *"I will give power unto My two witnesses and they shall prophesy 1260 days....and when they shall have finished their testimony, the beast that ascends out of the bottomless pit shall make war against them and shall overcome them,"* Revelation 11:3,7. Early in the last seven years, we flee from urban areas when we see what Christ said, *"the abomination of desolation* [military?] *standing where it ought not,"* Mark 13:14. Early Christians fled when they saw the Roman army coming. For us, it may mean martial law. Not to flee could mean you are picked up in the dark of night and sent to a detention center for screening and processing. Fleeing is preferred and is also represented by "scattering" in Daniel 12:7 and Zechariah 13:7.

2. *"And power was given him to continue 42 months,"*

Revelation 13:5. This is when the New World Order beast ascends. The papacy will be the woman on the beast for the second 3½ years, riding, guiding and controlling it as shown in Revelation 17. Before Global government is set up, they may say, "If you want to keep the Jewish Sabbath, go where the Jews are." That will be an opportunity represented also by Rev 12:14— "*To the woman were given two wings of a great eagle that she might fly to the wilderness.*"

"*Sell What You Have*"

This is so you can get something for your investment, because if you don't sell by this fall, 2015, economic collapse may mean you never will recover your investment. We need to integrate the Bible models suggesting we flee with these promises of what God is going to do. "*Sell what you have*" is His preface to the amazing promise, "*He will make* [us] *ruler over all that He has*," Luke 12:44. It doesn't mean we are homeless; we can rent, but it allows more mobility to respond to God's call.

In the hereafter, IAUA will make it up to those who presently give the best of their time, effort and resources for His cause. It will soon be too late. After the earthquake in Revelation 8:5, it follows in verse 7 that "*all green grass was burnt up.*" Moreover, the Bible says, "*as the flower of the grass, so shall the rich man fade,*" James 1:9-11, AKJV.

So we can give our money, time and effort to God's cause

of *present truth* right now and be blessed, or hold it, lose it later and be cursed! "*Bring all the tithes into the storehouse that there may be meat in mine house, and prove me now herewith, says IAUA of hosts, if I will not open you the windows of heaven, and pour you out a blessing, that there shall not be room enough to receive it,*" Malachi 3:10. This blessing is for now, because it has this end-time context:

"*IAUA, whom you seek, shall suddenly come to His temple, even the messenger of the covenant, whom you delight in: behold, He shall come, says IAUA of hosts. But who may abide the day of His coming and who shall stand when He appears? For He is like a refiner's fire...*" Malachi 3:1-3.

When money is not used to help the cause of God, "*they shall go into the holes of the rocks, and into the caves of the earth and....cast his idols of silver and his idols of gold, (which they made each one for himself to worship) to the moles and to the bats,*" Isaiah 2:19,20. This is why Christ said, "*Sell what you have and give alms,*" Luke 12:33.

Down-sizing with a move from city locations to secluded rural places would be an important first step toward readiness for when IAUA [via New World Order?] will give us the wings of an eagle. It would be better to consolidate your debts tied to a city location and have a secluded cabin or trailer debt-free on land with water that can grow a garden. God's first lessons were in a garden; time for more lessons!

Harmony with these biblical words: *"Flee...Scatter...Sell"*

1.   *"When you see the abomination...standing where it ought not...flee,"* Matthew 24:15.

2.   *"You shall flee as you fled from before the earthquake..."* Zechariah 14:5.

3.   *"When He shall have accomplished to scatter the power of the holy people,"* Daniel 12:7. This starts when *"Judgment must begin at the house of God,"* 1 Peter 4:17. The Greek word for judgment is *krisis*.

4.   *"Sell what you have...let your loins be girded and lights burning...that when He comes and knocks,* [earthquake] *you may open immediately..."* Luke 12:35,36.

In this text, we are behind schedule. *"Sell what you have"* is an opening statement. This suggests we may not fully understand the rest until we comply with the first part.

"Let this mind be in you which was also in Christ IAUshua, who, being in the form of God, thought it not robbery to be equal with God, but made Himself empty," Philippians 2:5-7.

To sell what we have is contrary to human wisdom. Most Christians seem to think that the more we have, the more influence we have. Paul said that he knew how to be abased and how to abound. Our nature loves abounding, but do we know how to be abased?

In the Judgment, it would be better to have been too eager to obey and done so prematurely, than to have delayed until it was too late! It might be too late now, but God knows our hearts and if we "put it on the altar," asking Him to sell it if He will, we've done what we could. But let's not hold out for top dollar. I've lived to regret an offer I had that seemed too low, but later I lost it all when the bank wouldn't refinance it.

"*Sell what you have*" is *present truth* for God's people now. One of the principles in Scripture is to move forward in the right direction, even if you can't see your way to the end yet. In going to the Promised Land in Joshua's day, the leadership had to put their feet into the water before it parted, and those things were written as lessons for us.

Timing

In Israel's history, there were three decrees that provided for their return from Persia: first by Cyrus, later by Darius, and finally by Artaxerxes. Going to the Promised Land in end-time is God's plan as He deals with earthly rulers who think they can hold their dominion in spite of His plan.

Seven times Moses told Pharaoh, "*Thus saith IAUA, God of Israel, Let my people go*," Exodus 5:1-10:3. Seven times [seven years] Nebuchadnezzar was humbled, Daniel 4:16. God will humble the earthly governments until they release those who choose to go to the land that He gave to Abraham. "*And if ye be Christ's, then are ye Abraham's seed, and heirs according the promise.*" Our position must be like an army in time of war, ready to move and to go where directed.

In Bible times, "*the commandment to restore and to build Jerusalem,*" Daniel 9:25, was a provision for God's people to return. We should expect Zechariah 14:1-3 soon with damage to Jerusalem and an opportunity to participate in rebuilding as in Bible times.

This also fits what God told Abraham at Passover when he gave his guests unleavened bread. "At this set time" [*mo'ed*] next year Sarah will have a son. Isaac was the son of promise representing God's end-time people who will also be born at Passover to a Christian church as barren as was Sarah.

The Feast of Unleavened Bread, or Feast of Weeks (seven weeks leading to Pentecost, Deuteronomy 16:10) is a supper of betrothal for us to become the spiritual bride of IAUshua. After covenanting to be His, we become inseminated with His law (Pentecost?) and are birthed as Isaac the following Spring. This results in a son of promise that Satan is ready to devour (Revelation 12:4?)

"*I will take you from among the heathen, and gather you out of all countries, and will bring you into your own land. Then will I sprinkle clean water upon you, and ye shall be clean...A new heart also will I give you, and ...I will put my spirit within you, and cause you to walk in my statutes, and ye shall keep my judgments, and do them. And ye shall dwell in the land that I gave to your fathers; and ye shall be my people, and I will be your God,"* Ezekiel 36:24-28.

The pope has already issued his *Dies Domini* letter to governments urging the enforcement of Sunday laws with violators to be prosecuted as heretics. We should appeal for religious liberty for Jews and Sabbatarians to worship God according to their conscience. This should get a ticket to Israel for all who choose to go, compliments of Uncle Sam who fulfills Bible prophecy with the *"wings of a great eagle,"* Revelation 12:14.

Logistics

How will we then live? After God *"gathers* [us] *out of all countries ...into* [our] *own land,"* Ezekiel 36:24. Ezekiel 37 shows dry bones coming together. A stick for Israel (10 tribes scattered to Europe and dispersed to America) represents Christians who accept the *torah* as the law of His kingdom, and a stick for Judah (Jews who accept the Messiah) "become one in mine hand...and David my servant shall be king over them says IAUA," Ezekiel 37:24.

"The days come, saith IAUA, that I will raise unto David a righteous Branch, and a King shall reign and prosper, and shall execute judgment and justice in the earth," Jeremiah 23:5.

Before David ascended the throne, he was tested and tried by a wilderness experience, similar to when Israel left Egypt. He lived in caves with bands of followers. The Bible seems to suggest that we may also have our wilderness experience: *"There be four things which are little upon the earth, but they are exceeding wise; the ants are a people not strong, yet they prepare their meat in summer; the conies [small mountain rabbits] are a feeble folk, yet make their houses in the rocks; the locusts have no king, yet they go forth by bands; the spider takes hold with her hands, and is in kings' palaces,"* Proverbs 30:24,26.

The sixth seal ends with kings and rich men hiding in dens and rocks. Maybe caves will be a welcome protection from nuclear holocaust or a serious increase in geo-engineered climate destruction caused by man's foolishness. Nuclear explosion could be suggested by *"the heaven departed as a scroll when it is rolled together,"* Rev 6:14. It is also suggested by the bitter waters from Wormwood, a word translated in Russian as Chernobyl where they had a nuclear accident.

This brings us back to the primary message of the earthquake and seals: *"Fear God..."* If we fear Him, we won't fear man and we may be free to go in the direction that others would fear. The roar of an old lion sends the herd in the direction of young lions on the hunt. We must abandon the herd instinct and go toward to roar of the **Lion of Judah**. The point here is not to give answers that aren't sure, but to realize there are questions that only God can answer—and He will, if we are seeking to conform our lives to Holy Scripture.

The remnant need to understand something about "*the time of Jacob's trouble*," Jeremiah 30:7. First we should understand the historic event. Jacob had gotten the birthright by deception and fled from Esau. But now he was directed by God to return to the Promised Land. Messengers said Esau was coming to meet him with 400 armed men and Jacob was not prepared for battle. He divided his company so that if they were attacked, some might escape, and he went alone to pray that night, to seek help from God.

Jacob's bitterest thought was that his own sin brought this danger to his company who were innocent. As he bowed in distress upon the ground with all that was dear at a distance, he felt a hand upon him. In the darkness the two wrestled for the mastery, but Jacob's mind was upon his sin and guilt that seemed to shut him out from God. Nevertheless, he clung to God's promises as his heart reached out for mercy.

At daybreak the stranger touched Jacob's thigh and it was put out of joint. Jacob then knew he was wrestling against superhuman strength and he pled, "*I will not let you go unless you bless me*." Through humiliation, repentance, and self-surrender, Jacob prevailed. His name was changed to 'Israel' which means "*ruling with God*." God miraculously changed Esau's heart from revenge to forgiveness after Jacob saw the folly of his own efforts to bring about what God would have accomplished in His time.

As Jacob had this "time of trouble" when he was going to the Promised Land in obedience, the remnant may have a similar experience. Jeremiah 30:3,7 blends these concepts. Satan will try to terrify the remnant with the idea that their situation is hopeless. But like Jacob, they will need to remember God's promises and their previous repentance, just as Jacob had previously repented.

The issues at stake may be more than we can understand now. Leviticus 16 describes the Day of Atonement that is a type of Judgment Day. Though Israel had previously confessed their sins and repented, they were required to fast and pray while Aaron went into the Most Holy Place before the ark with its mercy seat representing God's throne. Afterward Aaron came out and transferred Israel's sin to the scapegoat representing Satan. The goat was taken by a "fit man" into the wilderness, never to return.

The "fit man" represents the remnant who will not dishonor God at this strategic time. God is staking the honor of His kingdom on a group of people who show that His law is fair and can be kept. Satan tries to overthrow their faith just as he tempted Christ in the wilderness. If the remnant lose faith, it would be like the fit man letting the goat escape so that it finds its way back to camp heaped with the sin that was placed on it to defile God's people...

The fit man represents the remnant who wrestle with God at a time when they feel like saying as Christ, "*My God, why have you forsaken me?*" But like Jacob or Job, they hold on.

The issues at stake could be more serious than we realize. Satan has claimed God is unfair in making a law that cannot be kept, and that everyone else in history has sinned when times got tough. IAUshua kept the law, but Satan claims He was not really human like us. In the end, our Savior is depending on the remnant, the "fit man," to live in obedience when times are at their worst. They would rather die than commit sin and they vindicate God in showing His law is fair. They fulfill the imagery of the fit man that takes the goat into the wilderness.

This is why IAUshua is willing to share His throne with them, because they play such a strategic role. Sharing His throne is parallel to Jacob's name, Israel—"ruling with God." But this strategic role may be the very source of their anguish in Jacob's time of trouble, to realize that they might in some way dishonor God and let the devil and his load of woe back to camp. Satan will afflict them with their own sense of unworthiness, just as he troubled Jacob with a memory of his sin.

Zechariah 3 focuses on this issue. Satan was resisting Joshua and claiming his sin disqualified him. Our High Priest says to Satan, "*IAUA rebuke you... take away the filthy garments from him...Behold I have caused your iniquity to pass*" and Joshua [high priest] was sealed, as the imagery of Zechariah 3 and 4 suggests. Jacob's time of trouble came when he returned to the Promised Land, and it may be when we face the most severe conflict, and even death as he did. The change of Jacob's name and the miter put on Joshua's head in Zechariah 3 are both imagery that must be ours in a sealing process that will be unique to the 144,000, the bride of Christ.

Until then, our past experiences in sin have left us with memory echoes of how good the beer, chocolate cake, pork chops, illicit sex or drugs were. These memories give us an answering cord of response that inclines us toward the wrong so that we are tempted to sin again. But in this sealing process, God blots out (not just pardons) our iniquity so that we no longer have those fond memories of things that overcame us in the past. And just as the high priest interceded for his people, we must also accept that role and intercede as we pass through succeeding roles of prophets ("the time of God's judgment is come") and priests (a role of intercession) before becoming kings with Him, Revelation 1:6.

The 7th Seal ~ The Godhead

"And when he had opened the seventh seal, there was silence in heaven about the space of half an hour. And I saw the seven angels which stood before God....Jerusalem...mother of us all," Revelation 8:1,2; Galatians 4:26.

Music: Sweet Holy Spirit,

http://www.youtube.com/watch?v=-UG_hqlnePA

Outline

1. Overview and Trinity

2. Made in IAUA's image

3. Translation Problems

4. "Jerusalem, Mother of us all"

5. Daughter of Jerusalem; Key of David

6. Song of Solomon and Mary, a Surrogate

7. Virgins

Overview and Trinity

We are made in God's image male and female. Genesis 1:26-28; 5:1,2. Paul wrote, "*the invisible things of [God]...are understood from things that are made,*" Romans 1:20.

Just as a worm can become a butterfly, God is able to assume the form of the Spirit that can be everywhere, and "*Jerusalem which is above is the Mother of us all,*" Galatians 4:26.

Cities are named for persons and there is a "*family in heaven,*" Ephesians 3:15. Christ is the only begotten Son, John 3:16, but the Daughter of Jerusalem "*is the only One of her Mother,*" Song of Songs 6:9.

2 Kings 19:21,22 and Isaiah 37:22,23 show that She (Daughter of Jerusalem) was blasphemed. Blasphemy is a sin of speaking against God. And the next morning, 185,000 Assyrians were dead outside the city. She was God. Do we worship God? God is One in the sense that He is all loving, wise, good and has one purpose, but the word for *"one"* in Deuteronomy 6:4 is echad and it means a combined unity, just as the evening and

morning make one day, and a man cleaves to his wife and becomes one flesh, God is also a combined unity, *echad*.

To say that God is male only may contribute to abuse of wives worldwide by men who do not know that their wives are also made in the image of God. We now consider a view that helps our respect for half the human race.

The first 2000 years of earth's history ended with a Flood for those who rejected the Father. The 2nd 2000 years ended with a rejection of the Son. And if we finish the 2000 years since the cross by rejecting the Holy Spirit (of Truth), it will be trouble for us.

As numerous churches came from the mother church, they made various reforms, but the doctrine of the Trinity, boasted by the papacy as the foundation of all their belief, has not had much scrutiny by mainline Protestant churches.

There are seven references to "Daughter of Jerusalem" in Hebrew Scripture; some imply Deity as we will see.

This information does not fit the classic doctrine of Trinity. We've been conditioned by more than a millennium of papal teaching. The papacy even made war on three Arian kings that didn't accept its Trinitarian doctrines, Daniel 7:24. The imagery of a woman is used to represent a church; a pure woman represents God's church, an impure woman represents a false church. The Bible calls the impure woman *"the Mother of…Abominations,"* Revelation 17:5. The word "trinity" is not found in Scripture.

Made in IAUA's Image

Seven is God's signature. Truths emphasized <u>seven times</u> in Scripture are truths for end-time. From page 1 in the Bible "God [*Elohim* is the plural form of "God" in Hebrew and it has a feminine base, *Eloha*]…God said:

1. *"Let us make man <u>in our image,</u>*

2. <u>*after our likeness*</u>*…*

3. *So God* [Elohim] *created man <u>in</u>* [Their] *<u>own</u> <u>image,</u>*

4. *<u>in the image of God</u> created* [They them]

5. *male and female created* [They] *them....*

6. *In the day that God* [Elohim] *created man, in the likeness of God made* [They them]

7. *Male and female created* [They] *them,"* Genesis 1:26,27; 5:1,2.

Hebrew Poetry

God did not need to tell us we are "male and female," that is obvious. Scholars say the above is typical of Hebrew poetry, not with rhyming sounds, but with parallel ideas. Genesis 1:27 is an example. "Male and female" tells us how we are made in 'Their' image. If we are male and female and in 'Their' image, they too, are male and female. We were made in the image of God who also has hands and feet [Exodus 24:10,11], a mouth [Numbers 12:8], a heart [Hosea 11:8], and *"the hair of His head was white as snow,"* Daniel 7:9. Christ said, *"If you have seen Me, you have seen the Father,"* John 14:9.

Paul says, *"The invisible things of (Him)...are clearly seen, being understood from the things that are made, even*

His eternal power and Godhead," Romans 1:20. There is no Greek word for Him; it is supplied by translators who wrote what they understood from traditional teaching, but from the context of the Godhead, it should be Them. This says we can understand the invisible Godhead from the things that are made, male and female.

Young children can understand that father and mother, boys and girls, are all made in the image of a heavenly Father and Mother, but learned theologians have difficulty understanding this.

Translation Problems

The Hebrew words for God are El, Eloah and Elohim. El is masculine. <u>Eloah is the feminine form</u> that is correctly translated "Goddess." *Strong's* and *Englishman's Concordance* both show Eloah, not El, <u>is the root of Elohim,</u> the plural word for God used 2605 times throughout the Old Testament.

We have been misled by Bible translators whose views were shaped by Catholic doctrine of the Trinity. The Greek text has ***no male pronoun*** <u>to support these</u>

italicized words:

"The Spirit of truth; whom the world cannot receive, because it sees <u>Him</u> not neither knows <u>Him</u>: but you know <u>Him</u>; for <u>He</u> dwells with you and shall be in you," John 14:17.

Using a concordance, you will find no *"him"* or *"he"* — there are no Greek words to support "him" or "he" anywhere in Scripture for the Holy Spirit, but translators added the "he" and "him."

"Honor your Father and your Mother"

The first table of stone had the commandments showing our duty to God. In Jewish liturgy, the first table included "Honor your Father and your Mother..."

Paul reminds us that *"Jerusalem which is above is the Mother of us all,"* Galatians 4:26. A city cannot be our mother, but Jerusalem is named after Her, just as Washington, Lincoln, or Jefferson are cities named as a memorial for people.

The Name of the Holy Spirit

We have learned the names of the heavenly family—first the Father, then the Son, now the heavenly Mother. This enables us to do what Christ said in His parting words: *"Go therefore, and teach all nations, baptizing them in the name of the Father, and of the Son, and of the Holy Spirit,"* Matthew 28:19.

In the end-time, we are in danger of having a vain religion with empty words if we fellowship where they say, "I baptize you in the name of the Father, and the Son and the Holy Ghost," yet Their names are not known, used or appreciated.

IAUshua was telling us that we need Their names, but in our ignorance we've been slow to understand. We've seen Her name is Irushalem (there is no "J" in Hebrew; translators substituted J's for yods which, as vowels, had the "ee" sound). Our heavenly Mother is personified in Proverbs:

"Wisdom is the principal thing; therefore get wisdom, and with all thy getting, get understanding; exalt Her and She shall promote thee; She shall bring thee to

honor, when thou dost embrace Her; She shall give to thine head an ornament of grace; a crown of glory shall She deliver to thee; take fast hold of instruction; let Her not go; keep Her, for She is thy life," Proverbs 4:7-9,13.

God could have spelled everything out in the first few chapters of the Bible, but He wants us to "read between the lines," as searching for hid treasure. When Isaac asked where the lamb was for a sacrifice, Abraham said, *"God will provide Himself a lamb for a sacrifice,"* Genesis 22:8. Abraham, the father of the faithful, typified God because he was willing to sacrifice his son as the Lamb for our sins. From Moses to IAUshua, there is much between the lines of Scripture that we have missed. Could there be more? Yes, there's more! Who of us could claim that we fully comprehend even one verse of Scripture?

Paul refers to *"the whole family in heaven,"* Ephesians 3:15. A family is defined as parents and their offspring.

Just as a man would like to have a son to bear his image and name, God has given women similar instincts:

Jerusalem has a daughter, the *"Daughter of Jerusalem... Daughter of Zion,"* who is the Holy One in 2 Kings 19:21,22 and Isaiah 37:22. These texts support that She, too, is Deity...

Sennacherib, the king of Assyria, had destroyed every other army and was now mocking Israel's God at the gates of Jerusalem. Israel's king, Hezekiah, was afraid; he dressed in sackcloth to appeal for God's help and he sent Eliakim to the prophet Isaiah for counsel. Note the return message via Eliakim concerning Sennacherib...

*"**The daughter of Zion** has despised thee, and laughed thee to scorn; the daughter of Jerusalem has shaken her head at thee, **Whom thou hast reproached and blasphemed**,"* 2 Kings 19:21,22.

Blasphemy is a sin of speaking against God irreverently; the Daughter of Zion, the Daughter of Jerusalem was saying Sennacherib blasphemed Her. This is a clear statement that She is God. And She proved it; the next morning there were 185,000 dead Assyrians outside the city!

Eliakim, the messenger, must have understood Her role as Deity, and evidence suggests this is a key: "*The key of the house of David will I lay upon his* [Eliakim's] *shoulder; so he shall open, and none shall shut; and he shall shut, and none shall open*," Isaiah 22:20,22.

This "key of David" shows up again in Revelation 3:7 where the Holy Spirit opens the door to the Most Holy Place for the church of Philadelphia [brotherly love]. The Most Holy Place was where the Ark was kept; it represented the throne of God. Those who have this understanding can, by faith, see that we are made in IAUA's image, male and female. Reverence for the image of God in women is a deterrent to abuse or sexual sin that plagues the papacy.

We quote the text, "*he that cometh to God must believe that He is, and that He is a rewarder of them that diligently seek Him*," Hebrews 11:6. We should also be able to read it, "*he that cometh to God must believe that She is, and that She is a rewarder of them that diligently seek Her.*" It may bother us at first, as if we are adding something; but it was the translators who added the "he" and we see clearly we are made in Their image, and the root word used most often for God is feminine! Rabbis regard the Shekinah, the Holy Presence dwelling in light over the Ark in the Most Holy Place, as feminine.

Song of Songs

Scholars say the Song of Solomon is one of the least understood books in the Bible. They forget that as Israel's wisest king, Solomon typified Christ, and he was reflecting the spiritual truth of Christ's love for His Sister to whom He is betrothed: "Open to me, *my sister, my love, my dove, my undefiled*," Song of Songs 5:2. The Holy Spirit [His Sister, Dove] descended at His baptism, Matthew 3:16, and will be His Bride when He comes, Matthew 25:6; 22:2; Revelation 19:7. "*My spouse,*" is found six times in the Song of Solomon and suggests Their betrothal in heaven, the blossoming of a love born in eternity—

"The LORD possessed Me in the beginning of His way, before His works of old. I was set up from everlasting, from the beginning....When there were no depths, I

was *brought forth* [child birth, Strong's Concordance]...Then I was by Him, as one *brought up with Him: and I was daily His delight, rejoicing always before Him*," Proverbs 8:22-30.

Christ and His betrothed loved each other in heaven, but They put marriage on hold and covenanted to save us when our first parents sinned. She spoke of Her love for Him—"*Tell me, You whom my soul loves, where You feed, where You make Your flock to rest at noon: for why should I be as one that turns aside by the flocks of Your companions?*" Song of Songs 1:7. She would have preferred to be with Him in heaven, but would not leave us orphans [see John 14:18, margin]. She stayed with us, the flock. This is **the greatest love story ever told!**

Mary a Surrogate?

The most popular verse in the Bible says, "*God so loved the world that He gave His only begotten son,*" John 3:16. Traditional teaching has numbed us to the meaning of *"begotten."* The Greek words are *mono* [only or one] and *genes* [genetic, generate, procreated]. He could not be the <u>Divine Son</u> of God if He were not begotten—heaven is filled with angels that the Bible calls *"sons of God."* Adam was a son by creation, and fallen man by adoption, but IAUshua is the only begotten Son.

For IAUshua to be the *same* Divine Son on earth as He was in heaven, it would seem that He needed to have the *same* genes. The Bible teaches He was begotten by the Father and *"that which is conceived in [Mary] <u>is of the Holy Spirit</u>,"* Matthew 1:20. This suggests Mary was a surrogate, a concept now well understood. She provided flesh and bones, a human nature so Christ could be hungry, thirsty, tired—*"He took not on Him the nature of angels, but the seed of Abraham,"* Hebrews 2:14. He *"was in all points tempted like as we are, yet without sin,"* Hebrews 4:15,16. This information does not suggest that a male Holy Spirit had sex with Mary or impregnated her, but that a fertilized egg was implanted in her womb.

Christ had no advantage that we cannot have. He was

born of the Holy Spirit from birth. We may be born again and receive the Holy Spirit. Christ went to heaven and She is the one who says, *"I stand at the door and knock."*

"In the midst of the seven candlesticks <u>one</u> <u>like</u> unto the Son of man,...<u>girt about the paps</u> [Greek word is mastos, <u>female breast</u>] with a golden girdle...the seven candlesticks...are the seven churches...I stand at the door, and knock...hear what the Spirit says to the churches," Revelation 1:13, 20; 3:20,22.

When we give our lives to Them, the Holy Spirit comes and abides in us to *"guide [us] into all truth,"* John 16:13.

Nowhere does Christ say the Spirit is male. He implied to the contrary, but some translations mislead us with the word *"comfortless"* in John 14:16. <u>Christ is male and has begotten us spiritually, but would not leave us "orphans" [the Greek word is *orphanos*]. He left us the other [female] parent and She nurtures us as mothers do</u>:

"The Spirit also helps our infirmities: for we know not what we should pray for as we ought: but the Spirit

itself [Herself because the Greek is only neuter] *makes intercession for us with groanings* [of heartbreak when we sin] *which cannot be uttered,*" Romans 8:26.

Further support comes when we consider that the messenger [pastor] to the last of the seven churches is said to be blind and naked. *Naked* means the loins are not girded with truth, Ephesians 6:14. Why does the "True Witness" who is outside knocking say we are blind? We're blind because we don't recognize who's knocking...She, "*girt about the paps*" [*mastos,* female breast] is the One walking among the candlesticks [churches] in Revelation 1-3.

The words "he" and "his" in Revelation 1:14-18 were added by translators. There are no Greek words for "he" or "his" in these texts.

Some forms of nature, like a caterpillar later becoming a butterfly, may help us understand the Holy Spirit's ability to assume bodily form as well.

New Covenant Promise

Those who go to Israel when God "gathers [us] out of all countries" will get a double portion of the Spirit as Christ had when He was baptized. *"A new heart will I give you, and a new spirit will I put within you...and cause you to walk in my statutes, and you shall keep my judgments, and do them. And you shall dwell in the land that I gave to your fathers,"* Ezekiel 36:24-28.

It is easier to believe we are made in Their image if we understand that Jerusalem is the name of the Holy Spirit, and that She is "mother of us all." Through history, She has identified closely with God's people so that, speaking of the end time when the New Covenant is fully active, She— *"Jerusalem shall dwell safely* [with us] *and this is the name whereby She shall be called the LORD, our righteousness*," Jeremiah 33:16. If Jerusalem were only a city, it would not be called "the LORD." "She" is used in AKJV.

God's Name is a Clue

The letters of God's name, yod, hay, vav, hay may be understood to represent each member of the heavenly family. The yod means hand and represents our heavenly Father reaching out to save us. The hay means window and represents the Holy Spirit Mother— Jerusalem is Her name, Galatians 4:26. The vav means hook or nail and represents IAUshua who was nailed for us. The second hay represents the *"Daughter of Jerusalem,"* first mentioned in 2 Kings 19:21, Isaiah 37:22, also called Daughter of Zion and the Holy One of Israel. She is IAUshua's Bride.

This information suggests that Christ's parables on the marriage [the 10 virgins in Matthew 25:1-13, the King's marriage for His Son in Matthew 22:2-12, and His return from the wedding in Luke 12:35-37] all involve us as participants. We are invited as guests or attendants to the marriage. While in a spiritual sense we may be wed to Christ, the guest model suggests there is also a *"bride."*

"The Spirit (Mother) and the Bride (Daughter) say, 'Come," Revelation 22:17. Would we be inviting ourselves to our own wedding? The New Jerusalem city

is like a wedding gift He has prepared for Her and us!

The King's Daughter

"The king's daughter is all glorious within," Psalm 45:13.
*This cannot be speaking of any human—our
righteousness is as "filthy rags," Isaiah 64:6. *The margin
refers to Revelation 19:7,8—"*the marriage of the Lamb
is come, and His Wife has made Herself ready.*" She is
the King's Daughter! As Jacob worked seven years for
Rachel, it will be 7,000 years before the consummation
of the great controversy and Their marriage.

She is the Shekinah, the Presence of Light on the mercy
seat of the Ark in the Most Holy Place representing the
throne of God. *"Let us therefore come boldly unto the
throne of grace, that we may obtain mercy,"* Hebrews
4:15:16.

May God heal us from viewing women as sex objects.
Christ said, "*Blessed are the pure in heart, for they shall
see God*" (and not be destroyed), Matthew 5:8.

If we understand that we are a part of the **heavenly**

family that is not some queer arrangement [male Father, male Son, male Holy Ghost, with no feminine counterparts] we may have the boldness of Hebrews 4:15,16.

Throughout history men's egos have blinded them to many things. The papal view of an all- male Godhead is an example. God's crowning act, they say, was His creation of man. But women could easily argue that in the line of creation from fish and birds to mammals and man, Eve came last and was made out of better material than man!

Isaiah's vision of a celestial feminine Deity could be a reason for his response, "*I am undone*," Isaiah 6:5. Accepting the possibility of feminine Deity may be necessary for us to receive a vision of God as Isaiah did. "He that comes to God must believe that [S]he is," Hebrews 11:6. There is no word for "He" in the text. We believe He is; we should also believe She is!

The confessions of God's servants in Scripture when given a vision of Deity include an admission that they were unclean. Christ said, *"Blessed are the pure in heart, for they shall see God."* For a man who is not pure to see a loving, kind, beautiful woman would be sin for him if he wrongfully desires Her. We must be pure in heart in order to live in Their presence and not be consumed with lust. We should join David in his prayer, *"Create in me, O God, a pure heart..."* Those who stand in God's Presence will be pure.

To aid in a quest for purity, a vegetarian diet without the cholesterol, grease, blood or hormones favors better health, mental clarity and control of sexual desire. The diet that God chose for Israel in the wilderness on the way to the Promised Land, even though He could [and once did] provide for them flocks of quail, it otherwise did not include flesh. This was for health and also for self-control.

"Virgins" Revisited

Speaking of His return, Christ said, *"Elias truly shall come first and restore all thing,"* Matthew 17:11. Elijah was translated without dying and he was also single, like

John the Baptist and Christ.

The special group that receive the seal of His name—the 144,000 are also _virgins_ in Revelation 14:1-5. They are privileged to follow Christ wherever He goes. How do we become virgins?

Paul wrote, "_the time is short: it remains, that both they that have wives be as though they had none,_" 1_Corinthians_ 7:29. References in Scripture to a "short time" suggest application to the end-time, seven-years.

"_When a man has taken a new wife, he shall not go out to war, neither shall he be charged with any business: but he shall be free at home one year, and shall cheer up his wife which he has taken,_" _Deuteronomy_ 24:5.

Horses in Bible times were for war. The four horses in Revelation 6 support this as a time for war.

Marriage disqualified one from battle (Gideon's time) and battle disqualified one from marriage. (Uriah) They are mutually exclusive in the law. The end-time is a time of battle, spiritual warfare, not a time for marrying or having children. [Matthew 24:19].

Uriah, one of the noblest soldiers in the Bible was summoned from battle to see David who gave him leave to spend the night at home. He responded, *"the servants of my lord are encamped in the open fields; shall I then go into my house, to eat and drink, and to lie with my wife?...I will not do this thing,"* 2 Samuel 11:11.

"All men cannot receive this saying, save they to whom it is given...there be eunuchs which have made themselves eunuchs for the kingdom of heaven's sake. He that is able, let him receive it," Matthew 19:11,12.

Sin began when Adam chose Eve over God. We can make God first now. *"Every one that has forsaken houses or brethren or father or mother or wife or children or lands for my name, shall receive an hundredfold and shall inherit everlasting life,"* Matthew 19:11,12,29

The Big Picture

If we were to listen to the devil, we would get the idea that God is unfair in making a law that no one can keep, and then condemning us to hell for breaking it. Christ came to show us how to live. He kept the law and in dying, He offers to credit His perfect life to our sinful record. This supports God as loving us and being merciful, but it does not answer Satan's charge of an unfair law, because maybe Christ had some advantage that is not available to us.

To answer these charges, God is going to stake the honor of His name and kingdom on a group of people who correspond to the "fit man" in Leviticus 16:21. They do not dishonor God by sinning at a time when things are at the worst. They are threatened with death. They endure hunger, weariness and delay, even living without marital love for the end-time period, much like Jacob was betroth to Rachel for seven years. We must patiently hold our tempers as we drag a balking goat that represents Satan away from the camp of Israel as the imagery in Leviticus 16 suggests.

Men, for the sake of earthly glory, have deprived themselves of the comforts of home and family, and have braved the elements, often risking their lives. Will we do it for Their glory? It will all be over soon, and what an amazing privilege to have lived for God! "To him that overcomes will I grant to sit with Me on My throne," Revelation 3:21. *AllelulA!*

Summary

Each day for the week of Unleavened Bread, we've been considering topics that we don't hear about in church because over the centuries, the Bible truths that we've considered that have a 7-fold emphasis, have been altered by church leaders who wanted to make it easy for us. This is why Christ saw the need of Elijah to come and *"restore all things,"* Matthew 17:11. We can have a part in that.

1. We've learned that God's name is not "Lord" and the Lord's name is not God. The tetragrammaton of the Hebrew letters, yod, hey, vav, hey, "consists of four vowels," according to Josephus, and the best information we have on their pronunciation is ee-ah-oo-ah, represented as IAUA where the "I" has the international "ee" sound. These are the essential vowels for all languages. God is lending His name to us for any words we pronounce—

let's not take His name in vain!

http://GodsName1stSeal.wordpress.com

2. We can marry Christ as Israel did [Exodus 19:5,6; Jeremiah 3:14] by making a covenant. Bible covenants were linked to 7's, like the 7 ewes that Abraham gave Abimelech. We give God the things the Bible emphasizes 7 times as a mark of end-time truth, solemnly swearing to be His and faithful to these topics of covenant. By making a covenant, we also become His kingdom, Exodus 19:5,6. **http://Covenant2ndSeal.wordpress.com**

3. Kingdom means dominion of a king and He has dominion by His laws. These are summarized in the book of Deuteronomy which has been recommended to read, even as Israel heard the words and sealed to it in Nehemiah 9:38; 2Kings 23:2,3. The statutes and judgments are emphasized 7 times in Ezekiel 20:11-24 and are a focus of Elijah who is to "*restore all things*," Malachi 4:4,5; Matthew 17:11. They were designed to guard the 10 Commandments as they reflect those principles. **http://GodsLaw3rdSeal.wordpress.com**

4. The statutes also enjoin annual Sabbaths that were designed to teach truths in the plan of salvation. There are 7 *"holy convocations"* in Leviticus 23: the 1st and 7th day of unleavened bread; Pentecost, the Feast of Trumpets, the Day of Atonement and the 1st and 8th day of the Feast of Tabernacles. We saw that the month is indicated by the thin crescent in the western sky after sunset. That evening and the next day is the New Moon Day. Then there are six days to work before the 7th day is the Sabbath. This may be reviewed about half way down the page at—

http://4thSealSabbaths.wordpress.com

5. Christ said, "*I am come in my Father's name,*" John 5:43. If His Father's name was Zeus, then they pronounce it right in Italy when they say, Yea Zeus, or Hey Zeus in Latin America. We say Gee Zus, but the best information, even encoded by Equidistant Letter Sequences in the Messianic prophecies, would be Yahshua, or as we have learned IAUshua where we consider the yod, hey and vav as vowels (#1 above). Christ was a Nazirite and we considered the 7-fold

blessing on Nazirites as an indication of God's desire for us. **http://ChristsName5thSeal.wordpress.com**

6. Seven times God told Abraham, I will give you this land. Paul said, *"If you are Christ's, you are Abraham's seed, and heirs according to the promise,"* Galatians 3:29. In the end-time, when New World Order compels false worship [Revelation 13:14-17], we can have freedom to worship according to the Bible in the land of the covenant until Antichrist comes. We then may also expect deliverance from Christ who comes on the white horse of Revelation 19:11.

http://PromisedLand6thSeal.wordpress.com

7. Seven times the Bible says we are made in God's image or likeness, male and female. The 7th Seal is about the Godhead, not a homosexual trinity as most churches believe. We looked at Biblical clues for the *"Daughter of Jerusalem"* who was blasphemed (a sin of speaking against God). The Song of Solomon is really about Israel's wisest King—IAUshua and His betrothed—*"My Sister, My love, My dove, My*

undefiled," Song of Songs 5:2. She is the one *"like the Son of man...girt about the paps,"* Rev 1:13. They have been betroth before our world began, and like Jacob was betroth to Rachel for 7 years, they are waiting for Their marriage 7000 years, and we can be part of the wedding! Rev 22:17. We also saw that the 144,000 are "virgins" and we looked at Bible support for being such or like Uriah who, in the time of battle, would not sleep with his wife. Paul said, *"the time is short...[let] they that have wives be as though they had none,"* 1Corinthians 7:29. **http://Godhead7thSeal.wordpress.com**

It would probably be impossible for most people to read the above links and get it all the first time, so don't feel bad to revisit often along with your reading of Deuteronomy, Chapters 4-32.

Once familiar with this material, the reader is encouraged to make a solemn vow to IAUA, asking for His Spirit to bless, guide, teach and protect us through the end-times, to the intent that we can live for God and represent His character of love and mercy as well as truth and judgment.

The above topics take 7 days, corresponding to a biblical wedding of a week [Genesis 29:27]. The 8th day would be a Sabbath, and would be appropriate for reading any part of Deuteronomy 4-32 that hasn't been finished and making a covenant. It is possible that God will bless those who are faithful in the Way that they know He is empowering them as promised in Revelation 11:3, or His power may await Pentecost (see 4th seal to review how to count it, about half way down). For Pentecost, a message will be posted at—

http://TheBridegroomComes.wordpress.com

If you have questions or I might be of help, email me. I will respond as I am able: Ruhling7@juno.com

www.ingramcontent.com/pod-product-compliance
Lightning Source LLC
Chambersburg PA
CBHW060232050426
42448CB00009B/1409